D0960338

THE STANDARD & POOR'S GUIDE TO SELECTING STOCKS

Finding the Winners and Weeding out the Losers

Michael Kaye

McGraw-Hill

New York   Chicago   San Francisco   Lisbon   London   Madrid   Mexico City
Milan   New Delhi   San Juan   Seoul   Singapore   Sydney   Toronto

1 2 3 4 5 6 7 8 9 0 DOC/DOC 0 9 8 7 6 5

ISBN 0-07-145084-X

This publication is designed to provide accurate and authoritative information in regard to the subject matter covered. It is sold with the understanding that the publisher is not engaged in rendering legal, accounting, or other professional service. If legal advice or other expert assistance is required, the services of a competent professional person should be sought.
> —*From a declaration of principles jointly adopted by a committee of the American Bar Association and a committee of publishers and associations.*

McGraw-Hill books are available at special quantity discounts to use as premiums and sales promotions, or for use in corporate training programs. For more information, please write to the Director of Special Sales, McGraw-Hill Professional, Two Penn Plaza, New York, NY 10121-2298. Or contact your local bookstore.

This book is printed on recycled, acid-free paper containing a minimum of 50% recycled, de-inked fiber.

Library of Congress Cataloging-in-Publication Data

To my mother, Muriel,
whose courage during her long illness
inspired all who knew her.

ACKNOWLEDGMENTS

THE IDEA FOR THIS BOOK CAME from the stock screen column that Numer DeGuia and myself write each week for Business Week Online. Our editor, William Andrews, informed us that it was a popular column on the website. With that knowledge, I recognized that there was not much published about stock screening.

This book would not have come about without the help and contributions of many individuals. First of all, I would like to thank Jim Dunn. Jim is a former treasurer of GTE and is presently a consultant for Standard and Poor's. He gave me multiple ideas on how to enhance the book and his input can be seen throughout the work.

I would like to thank my supervisors at S&P, Tom Gizicki and David Braverman, for encouraging me to write the book. David gave me a lot of advice from his own experience of writing his book *Standard & Poor's Guide to Saving and Investing for College.*

I would also like to acknowledge Jim Branscome, Jim Murphy, and Jean Kozlowski for reading over my manuscript. Their edits and advice helped produce a more polished final product. I am also grateful to the team at McGraw Hill and S&P, including Kelli Christiansen, Lisa O'Connor, Scott Kurtz, Stephen Isaacs, Shari Stein, Jeffrey Krames, and George Gulla for accepting my idea for the book, reviewing and enhancing the manuscript, and walking me through the production process.

I would like to thank my father, who has always taken great interest in me and my brothers' careers. Through some of his contacts, he helped me obtain finance-related internships while in college and my first real job on Wall Street.

Lastly, I would like to thank my wife, Emily, and my daughter, Megan. Emily taught me the value of time management. Her juggling of being a full-time attorney, a wife who actually cooks, and a terrific mother to our daughter made me realize that I could take on this project by budgeting my time. Most of all, I would like to thank my daughter, Megan, for providing the source of motivation for writing this book. She truly is the light of my own and my wife's lives and has helped us become better all-around people. I hope one day she will be proud of her father.

CONTENTS

INTRODUCTION: SCREENING FOR INVESTMENT WINNERS

L ET'S FACE IT—CHOOSING WINNING STOCKS is no easy task. There are over ten thousand equities publicly traded on the major U.S. stock exchanges. It is virtually impossible for individuals, and even for large brokerage firms' research staffs, to sift through the financial statements and public filings of all these companies to determine which stocks are best for them or their clients.

In the age of the Internet and personal computer, however, even new investors can access massive amounts of financial data that would have taken months or even years to compile less than a decade ago. The financial statements of all exchange-listed companies are available in many investment-related databases. With the click of a finger, this data can be sorted and sifted based on different investment characteristics. All an investor needs to do is determine what attributes they are looking for in a stock that they may be interested in purchasing. A similar approach can be used for picking suitable bonds or mutual funds. Best of all, many investment screening tools are available free of charge on many financial websites.

Most individual investors get their investment ideas and decide to buy stocks based on one of three basic reasons: (1) they get a recommendation from a broker, family member, or friend, (2) they have personal experience using a company's products or services, or (3) they see or read from the media that a company has a positive development. An investor may find a great stock by one of these methods, but there is probably a better chance the stock will be a loser.

Buying stocks based on a hot tip from a friend or family member is usually not a smart move. The source providing the information to your friend or family member may be questionable or have a hidden agenda. Moreover, the rationale given for purchase of the security is generally not thorough. The person providing the recommendation usually doesn't follow up and give an exit strategy or tell you when you should sell.

The hotter the tip, the more speculative it is likely to be. These are stocks that you are told have a good chance of doubling or tripling in value, when, in fact, there may be a bigger probability that you could lose a half to a third of your investment. One of investment's golden rules is in order to achieve large benchmark-beating returns you have to accept risk greater than the market. There is no free lunch. Brokers can be helpful in providing information and executing trades, but they also have a financial interest in giving you advice on specific stocks. After all, they make money from commissions when you purchase one of their recommendations through them.

The second most common way people choose stocks is through familiarity with the company. You assume that if you use and like a company's products or services, others must like them, too. The problem is that many people come to this conclusion without considering the firm's financial condition or competitive position.

The products of a company that you think are a great value may be a tremendous deal for consumers but not produce much profit to the company. Furthermore, the particular product you like could be a big money maker but might represent only a small fraction of the company's revenues. Even good companies with several successful products do not necessarily make good stocks. Sometimes strong companies can have stock valuations that are very expensive compared to what they can realistically expect to earn going forward.

A third main way investors choose their stocks is by the media reporting a positive news development for a company. For example, when a newscaster on television says that company X has a new potential blockbuster drug or company Y has a new revolutionary technological gadget, this will surely garner a lot of investor interest. The problem is that besides you, many other people will be simultaneously getting the same information. By the time the information is conveyed to the marketplace, there is a good chance that the stock may have moved already and not allow the investor to get a favorable price. These stocks tend to have most of the good news already reflected in the stock price. The stock market is usually very efficient in incorporating breaking news events into the price of a stock.

The main reasons why most people rely on these three methods for choosing stocks are habit, laziness, and that they do not have the knowledge or self-confidence to do it in other ways. They have always done it that way, and it requires very little effort on their part. Invariably, the stock tip from your brother-in-law or the stock-picking idea based on your own experience with a company will not take into account your tolerance for risk and your time frame. Even if it does, you should take the extra step and compare a stock with some of its peers and learn as much about the company as you can. In this day and age, tools are widely available at little or no cost that make the comparison easy. Unfortunately, a lot of people give more thought to where they want to go out to dinner on a Saturday night than they do to where they should invest their life's savings.

Stock screening or stock filtering is the process of finding equities that meet certain selected criteria. An example might be stocks traded on U.S. exchanges that have a market capitalization above five billion dollars, a forward price/earnings ratio below fifteen, and a three percent dividend yield. As more criteria are added, the more refined and selective the output becomes. It is important, however, to regard screening as an early quantitative step or "first cut" in the investment process. Once you have your screening results, the output should undergo further scrutiny and judgment by you, which you can accomplish on your own or by studying the analysis and opinions of a brokerage firm or an independent financial research company.

Screening is used in many other noninvestment-related fields. For example, in medicine, doctors give a series of tests to try to isolate what is ailing a patient. With each test, they try to narrow down what is causing the patient distress. Certain diseases and conditions are ruled out by the results from the tests. Each further test brings the physicians closer to determining what the possible illness is.

When searching for oil sites, explorers look for certain features in the topography of a specific region. An area has to pass certain criteria before actual drilling will begin. Lastly, in selecting students for admission, colleges and universities use the process of screening. Many top schools use filters to weed out students who do not have certain grade point averages or standardized test scores.

Unfortunately, as with potential securities, medical evaluations, drilling sites, and good prospective students, screening does not always result in a hundred percent success rate. Doctors are not always right with their diagnosis, oil drillers drill many dry holes, and universities select some students who end up performing poorly. Overall, though, the process of screening is essential for their work. It reduces a large universe of possibilities into a smaller and much more manageable universe.

Some financial screens are widely followed by the investment community. For example, the Dogs of the Dow is a screen that picks the ten highest yielding stocks in the Dow Jones Industrial Average at the start of the year. The Investors Business Daily Top 100 picks the hundred companies whose combined earnings growth and share price relative strength are the highest. Standard and Poor's Platinum portfolio combines stocks that are ranked highest by their fundamental analysts and their Fair Value quantitative model.

Screening used to only be available to professional portfolio managers with large financial resources. One needed a great deal of computer power and memory to take part in the process. Furthermore, the output of the screens was somewhat limited because the financial databases, which provide the backbone of a screener, were not very comprehensive. In recent years, culminating with the growth of the internet, increased electronic data storage capacity, and widespread computer use, high level screening has become available to the mass public.

Screening is one of the best ways for investors to get and test investment ideas. It is a tool that is widely available and is being used more and more by both individual investors and portfolio managers. Despite this, it is a subject about which there is not a lot written. Screening as a technique for investment selections is at its infancy. In the coming years, it is going to grow substantially and become much more widespread in its use by individual and institutional investors.

Before using a screen as an early step in their stock selection process, investors should know what it can and cannot achieve. Screening can help people become better investors by instituting greater discipline in their investment process. Successful investors establish a consistent approach and stick with it.

Screening allows an investor to be more objective and comparison shop when deciding whether to buy or sell a security. By using screening, an investor will have more of a sense of the stock that they are actually considering buying and will be less likely to be surprised by what happens to the stock after purchase. Screening is a tool that empowers individual investors and can help level the playing field between them and institutional investors. Individuals must be careful, however, because even the most advanced tools can do little good if not in the hands of one with a mastery of the tools capabilities and an intelligent strategy for implementing them.

Investing isn't rocket science. If individuals take the time to educate themselves a little, they can develop investment ideas by themselves. If investors, on the other hand, follow the crowd they can pretty much assure themselves of getting mediocre or sub par results. Screening allows investors to be proactive and more likely ahead of the curve.

In this book, we will explain various ways you can use screening to generate investment ideas for different kinds of investments and all the major investment styles. Screens can be easy enough for the neophyte and robust enough for the professional portfolio manager.

We try to explain all the concepts in the book in plain English, limiting the use of complex financial jargon, and making the book readable and useful for the typical investor. This book is most appropriate for individuals with some investment experience who are searching for ways to improve their investment results at little or no cost. It would be helpful for anyone looking for investment ideas including: individual investors, brokers, financial advisors, portfolio managers, trust officers, and treasurers.

Screening, like any other tool, cannot guarantee investment success. Some investments will increase more than one expects, and others will underperform. Any activity though that increases someone's chances of finding potentially good investments should be explored. Finance/investing is more than anything else an exercise in probabilities. In our opinion, screening is such an activity that increases one's odds for investment success.

In the early chapters, we'll look at what screening is and where to find the appropriate screening tools. We'll examine the strengths and weaknesses of the process. We'll discuss what financial data are available and useful to filter. Next, we'll show you how to screen for stocks, bonds, and mutual funds. Included are numerous examples of screens and an explanation of the themes that are commonly used in the screening process. Throughout the book, we'll talk about what steps an investor should take after developing a good list of stocks and other investments. In the later chapters, we mention how to reverse engineer the output from stock screens. Lastly, we'll discuss what the future trends in screening are likely to be and how the process of screening can make you a more knowledgeable and successful investor. If you have any questions or comments about the book, you can e-mail me at michael_kaye@sandp.com.

BOMBARDED WITH INFORMATION

> The difference between great people and others is largely
> a habit—a controlled habit of doing every task better,
> faster and more efficiently.
>
> —*William Danforth, founder, Ralston Purina*

W E ARE LIVING IN AN AGE where company and financial news is ubiquitous. We live in a 24/7, instantaneous information society. The sheer quantity of financial information is mind-numbing, making it impossible for an individual to absorb it all. There are cable television stations such as CNBC, CNNfn, and Bloomberg, which focus exclusively on business and financial news. *The Wall Street Journal, Financial Times,* and *Investors Business Daily* are daily newspapers geared toward investors. *Barron's* provides financial information and insight on a weekly basis. A great deal of the content of widely circulated magazines such as *Forbes, Fortune, Business Week, The Economist, Money, Kiplingers,* and *Smart Money* is investment-related. There are also financial newsletters, weekly investment-related public television shows such as *Wall Street Week,* and radio stations exclusively focused on business news. Brokerage and mutual fund companies will generally offer their clients some degree of access to their investment research and analysis. And finally, there is the all-encompassing Internet, where one can find news, financial statements, SEC filings, and opinions from all sorts of entities on every listed company on the major exchanges. Through the Internet, investors are also able to get access to Web broadcasts of a company's earnings releases. Overall, anyone who is willing to look for financial information can find it.

Often, in these various media sources, portfolio managers, analysts, and journalists give investment recommendations. This glut of information and advice for investors trying to make investment decisions can be intimidating and confusing. Sorting out the good advice from the bad is difficult. You may also get conflicting information. One supposed investment guru says that XYZ stock is a buy; others say they would not touch the stock with a 10-foot pole. It is rare that you see anyone saying anything negative about a company while it is at its 52-week high, or anything positive when it's at its 52-week low.

All in all, more information is better than less information. Not too long ago the amount of investment news was significantly more limited. In a lot of cases the stock tips investment pros gave to their clients or the media were biased. Often they were based on hidden agendas instead of true investment merit. For instance, stockbrokers might push to clients equities in which their firm had a large inventory that they wanted to get rid of. Besides large commissions, the brokers received perks such as free dinners, sporting events, and Broadway show tickets for being the best sellers of certain stocks and mutual funds.

Research analysts at brokerage firms covered companies that had high investment interest and were widely traded. In a lot of cases the research they provided was merely the regurgitation of what a company's management was providing them. Often they recommended stocks that their companies had large investment banking relationships with, regardless of the actual quality of the stock. An analyst suggesting that an investor should sell a stock when his or her firm was involved in the underwriting very rarely occurred. In some extreme cases, analysts who wanted to give negative stock recommendations to investment banking clients were terminated by their brokerage employer. Furthermore, almost all the recommendations from the brokerage community were either buy or hold. The number of sell recommendations was minuscule, leading many to interpret a "hold" recommendation to instead be a "sell" recommendation.

Recently, 10 of the largest investment banking/brokerage firms settled with the New York Attorney General's Office and agreed to pay $1.4 billion because the research they provided their clients was not independent and was subject to a number of conflicts of interest. Some well-compensated and followed analysts such as Jack Grubman and Henry Blodgett were publicly saying that certain telecom and Internet stocks were screaming "buys," but privately through their e-mails or other forms of correspondence were saying that the same stocks were not worth the paper they were written on. Coincidentally—or not—their firms had gigantic investment banking relationships with these companies that they were publicly praising.

Under the settlement with the government, the money the 10 firms pay will go toward investor restitution, fines, and independent research. Hopefully, this will serve as a wake-up call to the Wall Street research community to start acting more like research analysts and less like investment bankers and equity salesmen. When analysts and money managers talk about specific stocks on television and give buy or sell advice on the air, it is now more common for the reporter to ask them if there are any conflicts of interest. Sometimes, analysts even reveal if they have any affiliations with the "recommended" company without even being asked.

Overall, the outcome of the settlements has led to more independence and fewer conflicts of interest. Of course, this is a positive step. One has to wonder, however, whether these legal actions would have even taken place if not for the sharp decline in the stock market in 2000, 2001, and 2002. Other actions by the government, such as the formation of the Securities and Exchange Commission in the 1930s and the deregulation of brokerage commissions in the 1970s, occurred after steep drops in the stock market. When the stock market is going up, there isn't much scrutiny by investors. Everyone but the short sellers is happy. When the market has a big decline, though, investors are looking to assign blame and someone's head to fry.

Even in the near future, when brokerage research will hopefully be better and less biased, an analyst's generic recommendation is not going to take into account whether the investment is appropriate specifically for you. Will the investment advice incorporate what stage of life you are in, what your risk tolerance is, how this stock meshes with your other investments, what type of return you are hoping for, whether you have an aversion to a particular industry?

No two investors are exactly alike. They can have different attitudes toward money, be different ages and at different stages in life, have different family structures and incomes, different health circumstances and education levels, different values and attitudes toward risk and reward, just to name a few of the characteristics that make investors unique and what should make their portfolios different.

On average, the largest brokerage firms provide research on about 800 stocks. The trend in the future is for most of the large brokerage firms to provide fundamental research on fewer companies. On its own, investment research without investment banking, trading, and portfolio management fees is a cost center for a financial firm, not a profit center. This is a main reason why coverage will decrease.

The void left by the brokerage firms reducing their coverage will probably be filled by independent research providers who have no conflicts of interest with the companies they follow. Importantly, these firms vary widely in size, experience, and expertise. Furthermore, the vast majority of stocks listed on the exchanges will not be covered by analysts.

SCREENING TO SUIT THE INVESTOR

Screening is a way for individual investors and professional money managers to find some of the undiscovered gems not yet being followed by the large Wall Street firms. It's also a tool that allows investors to filter out what's important and what's not in choosing their specific investments. And it allows an investor to buy a security without having to be sold one. Screening is a great first step for investors to use to determine which stocks may be worth further inspection. It weeds stocks out that should not be considered in the first place. A recently retired investor may be interested in stable, high-yielding investments, while someone just starting out in his or her career may want to focus on fast-growing companies in emerging industries. Generally, younger investors can afford to buy more speculative issues in an attempt to achieve above average returns. They have time on their side.

FIGURE 1-1   Web sites with stock screeners.

www.aaii.com	www.moneycentral.msn.com
www.advisorinsight.com	www.morningstar.com
www.barchart.com	www.my.zacks.com
www.b4utrade.com	www.nasdaq.com
www.businessweek.com	www.pristine.com
www.cbs.marketwatch.com	www.quicken.com
www.clearstation.com	www.screen.yahoo.com
www.equitymodel.com	www.smartmoney.com
www.estrong.com	www.sixer.com
www.fidelity.com	www.stockworm.com
www.idayo.com	www.tdwaterhouse.com
www.incrediblecharts.com	www.troweprice.com
www.investors.com	www.valuengine.com
www.investor.reuters.com	www.wallstreetcity.com
www.marketscreen.com	

Screening is available on many different Web sites. Figure 1-1 provides a list of several Web sites that have screeners on them.

In the future, it's likely there will be many more financial Web sites with screeners on them. Each one of the screeners is unique. We encourage you to try to examine as many as you can. Throughout the book, we will provide examples of screens from these different screeners. We have reviewed numerous screeners and provided a layout of a sample screener in Figure 1-2. It has many of the data items that an investor would want to be able to mine.

FIGURE 1-2   Sample screener.

Universe

All Listed
Index
Industry
Subindustry

Liquidity Ratios

	min	max
Current Ratio	min	max
Debt/Equity	min	max
Cash/Total Assets	min	max
Long-Term Debt/Cash Flow	min	max

Share Data

	min	max
Price	min	max
Market Cap	min	max
Dividend Yield	min	max
Average Volume	min	max

Valuation Ratios

	min	max
	min	max
Price/Forward Earnings	min	max
Price/Sales	min	max
Price/Book Value	min	max
Forward PEG	min	max

Stock Performance

	min	max
1-week performance	min	max
1-month performance	min	max
3-month performance	min	max
1-year performance	min	max
5-year performace	min	max
13-week relative strength	min	max

Growth Rates

	min	max
1-year EPS Growth	min	max
5-year EPS Growth	min	max
Dividend Growth Rate	min	max

Sales and Profitability

	min	max
Sales Revenue	min	max
Profit Margins	min	max
ROE	min	max
ROA	min	max

Miscellaneous

	min	max
Institutional Ownership	min	max
Insider % Ownership	min	max
Debt Rating	min	max
Average Brokerage Rating	min	max

Search Now

CHARACTERISTICS OF SCREENERS

A useful and powerful screener will have many of the following characteristics:

Sufficient Data and Financial Ratios to Mine

First and foremost, a screener must have a large array of useful financial data that can be mined. Without this feature, a screener is not very helpful. The data items on the screener have to be measurable. If need be, an investor should be able to look back at a specific financial statistic in time (at least five years) to see what the value of the data item was. Besides having absolute financial values, it is important for the screener to have relative values. Showing that a company had $100 million in sales last year is not as powerful an argument to invest in a stock as a statistic showing that the company has been increasing sales each of the last five years. Relative values can help an investor identify a trend for a company.

Easy Web Site Navigation and the Option to Transfer Output to Other Applications

This is somewhat obvious. For the screener to be useful, it must be easy to move around and adjust the inputs. Ideally, the screener should come with some helpful instructions on how to best utilize it. Surprisingly, most screeners do not come with any instructions. It is also important to be able to save your self-created screens and be able to download the results to other software applications, such as Excel. Some even come with back tests showing how a certain screening strategy would have done in the past. Investors should be mindful that back tests are subject to the disclaimer in all financial products: past performance is no guarantee of future results.

Some Preset Screens

Preset screens have financial variables that are fixed by the provider. They provide a quick and easy way for investors to get some investment ideas. They eliminate the process of building a screen from scratch. Preset screens are especially useful for beginning investors before they get their feet wet creating their own screens. Usually, they include screens for the popular investment styles such as growth and value.

Outside Fundamental Rankings as a Filter

One of the main weaknesses of screening is that it is all numbers driven without any regard to qualitative features. A filter or two that includes outside analyst overall rankings partially alleviates this problem. Ideally, the analyst recommendations will include brokerage and independent research analysts. Fundamental analysts look at characteristics such as a firm's competition, product quality, and its customer loyalty, factors that cannot be measured quantitatively. If a company passes a bunch of quantitative filters with flying colors but the collective opinion of Wall Street analysts is a "sell" rating, the investor may want to take pause and investigate it further.

For example, Altria Group (formerly known as Philip Morris) generally looks great in terms of quantitative numbers such as sales growth, dividend yield, and cash flow. The reason outside analyst rankings are important in this case is because for Altria Group (MO) quantitative screens can never pick up the risk the company faces from the qualitative factor of smoking related litigation. With outside analyst rankings as a filter, this type of risk will hopefully be incorporated in the analysts' evaluations of whether the stock is a buy, hold, or sell. You should be aware that many fast growing companies are not followed by any analysts. Even when firms are covered by one or two analysts, it is not particularly meaningful in helping investors with their stock picking because it represents a very small sample.

Financial Ratios with a Range of Values, Not Just a Greater or Less Than Parameter

Allowing the user to insert a range of values makes for a better screener. It allows the investor to easily tighten the parameters for the screen and lessens the chance that outliers appear as output. For example, low price/earnings ratios are a staple of value screens. Having a filter to choose a historical P/E ratio, say, of "between 6 and 15" is much better than having a filter of an historical P/E ratio of "less than 15." With the second scenario, the screener is going to pick up companies that have negative P/E ratios. These stocks have not made money recently and probably were not the intended targets of the types of companies a value investor would be looking to invest in.

For screeners where one is not able to put in a range of values, investors need to be vigilant after getting their output to make sure that the stocks that appear satisfy the initial intent of the investor's screen. For instance, when an investor screens for stocks with a market cap below $1 billion with insider ownership above 50 percent, we do not believe he or she would be satisfied investing in a stock of a company that had a market cap of just $5 million whose insiders owned 95 percent of the shares outstanding.

Some Forward-Looking Ratios

Stocks are valued based on the discounted value of their future earnings stream. Not having some ratios that look forward will always give you a backward-looking bias. Historical ratios and statistics can be helpful, but investors get outsized returns by being right about what happens in the future. In the investing world, history doesn't always repeat itself. Investment styles that worked well in the past will not necessarily work going forward. A forward P/E and forward PEG ratio are two of the best forward ratios a screener can have.

A Glossary to Determine How the Ratios Were Derived

Explaining how the screener defines certain financial ratios is critical. For example, on virtually every screener there is a filter for price/earnings ratio. Unfortunately, very few of the sites say whether it is the forward or historical value that is being used. Yet this distinction is critical in determining the valuation of a company. Also, some financial data items such as cash flow and book value can have different definitions. It is imperative that investors know that the items they screen for are what they think they are.

KNOW THE RISK POTENTIAL

Investors often focus on the return potential of an investment. They should give even more attention to the potential risk. Before committing any dollars toward any security, an investor should be aware of the risks. Unfortunately, there are a lot of potential pitfalls for investments. Investors should know themselves and their ability to tolerate risk. To many investors, risk is simply the chance of losing a portion of their money. If holding a certain stock is keeping an investor up at night and giving him or her an ulcer, serious consideration should be given to selling it. No investment, whatever its return potential, is worth a toll on a person's health.

Before investors begin screening for investments, they should be aware of some of the forms of investment risk. Every security faces its individual security (unsystematic) risk. This risk comes from characteristics that are unique to the individual security. Factors such as the company's earnings growth, amount of debt, and prospects going forward are elements of security risk. By adding other investments to a portfolio, this type of risk can be reduced.

Market (systematic) risk is the risk of the security caused by actions in the overall market. If the overall market has a sharp decline, the individual stock is likely to decline as well. Actions by the Federal Reserve Bank, global events, inflation, and unemployment rates can affect the market as a whole and affect the individual securities that compose it. In other words, market risk cannot be diversified away by adding more securities; every investor is exposed to it.

Most investments face liquidity risk. The ability to convert a security into cash quickly and inexpensively is a primary concern of many investors. Active securities with large daily trading volumes and many interested buyers and sellers are the ideal, but not always the reality. In instruments such as high-yield bonds and micro cap stocks, liquidity can be a concern.

Inflation is another possible detriment to investments. Inflation erodes the purchasing power of consumers. Even if a security rises 10 percent in a year, if the inflation rate rises 15 percent, the investor loses. In recent years, inflation has been at low levels. In the coming years, there is no guarantee that it will remain tame. The U.S. Treasury recently began issuing Treasury Inflation Protected Securities (TIPS) for investors who are concerned about inflation risk. The principal on TIPS adjust with the consumer price index annually, providing a hedge against rises in inflation.

Whatever the investment choices you make as an investor, you should be aware of the types of risk you face. It is hard to take any kind of action to combat risk when you don't know what you're dealing with.

POINTS TO REMEMBER

▶ There are numerous sources for financial information, including the newspaper and television media, financial magazines, and the Internet.

▶ The quality and independence of the recommendations by financial professionals has been mixed.

▶ Screening is a tool that allows investors to better choose stocks based on characteristics that are important to them.

▶ Screening weeds out stocks that investors should not consider investing in.

▶ Screening is available on numerous financial Web sites.

▶ A good screener has many of these characteristics: (1) a large amount of data to filter, (2) easy navigation, (3) some preset screens, (4) outside fundamental rankings as one of the filters to choose from, (5) the financial ratios in the screener should have a range of values to put in, (6) some forward-looking ratios, and (7) a glossary.

▶ There is some kind of risk in all investments; some types can be reduced, others cannot.

WHY SCREEN FOR STOCKS?

A good trader has to have three things: a chronic ability to accept things at face value, to feel continuously unsettled, and to have humility.

—*Michael Steinhardt*

FOR SUCH A WIDELY available tool on financial Web sites, screeners generally come with few if any instructions. They do not state what they can and cannot do. The vast majority do not come with warnings about how they can be misused. Using screeners by no means guarantees that an investor will outperform the market. A poorly designed screen will provide companies that do not meet the investor's goals and objectives. There is no assurance that the output from a screener will provide the characteristics one initially screened for going forward. Although they are very helpful tools and should be utilized, screeners have some limitations.

A screener, in essence, has three parts: (1) a database of financial statistics for public companies, (2) a set of variables that you can filter, and (3) a screening engine that compares individual company statistics to the desired variables and subsequently generates a list of matches.

Screeners are only as powerful as the financial databases they use. If the database does not have a lot of ratios and figures, the screener will be of limited use. If there are mistakes in the database, it is possible you may get some incorrect results when you screen. Thomson Financial, Bloomberg, Reuters, and Standard & Poor's Compustat all provide comprehensive databases. It is important to realize that if the same screen is run on two different screeners, it is possible to get varying results because the amount of information in the databases may be different and they may be updated at different times. Screening is subject to the old maxim: garbage in equals garbage out.

As mentioned earlier, screening also has a backward-looking bias. Most of the financial information for the companies in the screeners is based on financial statements that can be three months to a year old. Recently listed initial public offerings and relatively new companies will not show up prominently in screening because of their lack of trading and financial history. When screening incorporates forward measures, it is putting a lot of weight into analysts' projections. The more long term the forecasted figures are for, the more difficult it is to predict and to be accurate. Overall, the output from screening is generally better suited for long-term investors than day traders who want to take advantage of perceived short-term market inefficiencies.

WHAT SCREENERS CANNOT MEASURE

Screening is driven by quantitative statistics. It is a rules-based and numbers-guided process. There are firm-specific qualitative measures that cannot be measured in a screen, such as:

- Quality of the company's management
- Customer loyalty
- Extraordinary items, such as potential lawsuits and real estate transactions affecting the company, pending patents, and the company's relationship with suppliers
- Macroeconomic factors, such as the level of interest rates, the inflation rate, the unemployment rate, gross domestic product growth, and the federal government's surplus or deficit

- Geopolitical factors, such as problems with a large trading partner, depreciation of a major currency, wars, and the threat of terrorism

These types of factors can have a significant effect on a specific stock and the overall market's future performance.

BENEFITS OF SCREENING

Despite some limitations, however, the benefits of screening are too powerful to ignore. In a matter of seconds, screening can take 10,000 possible stocks and narrow them down to 10 based on characteristics a particular investor is looking for. It clearly saves time for investors and portfolio managers looking for investment ideas. Screening is also offered free on many Web sites. Any product that is offered for free or at low cost and can help investors save time and improve their stock picking should be utilized.

Screening allows an investor to search for equities using both a bottom-up analysis and/or top-down methodology. A bottom-up manager conducts research on individual stocks and invests based on the underlying companies' financial fundamentals. A top-down manager examines broad economic trends, picks an industry, and then searches for companies within the industry to invest.

As noted earlier, screening instills discipline in the investment process. A company either passes a screening filter or it fails. If a screen is looking for stocks with market caps above $1 billion, any company with a market cap below this amount will not be included in the results. Screening puts each stock on equal footing. Since it is based primarily on numbers, it takes the emotion element out of the process. Strictly using screening helps investors avoid buying overhyped stocks. Furthermore, many investors hold on to a stock too long because it is considered a blue chip company, has a storied past, or it's a well-regarded household name. Screening helps investors identify stocks they have some kind of emotional attachment to but should sell once they no longer meet the parameters outlined in the screen.

Not using screening is equivalent to a baseball manager deciding on a pinch hitter without looking at the batting averages of the players he has on the bench. If you run the same screens periodically, it will give you new investment ideas of stocks to purchase. Also, if a stock falls out of a screen, it may give you reason to pause and investigate whether you still want to own it.

Screening is a great way to help people learn what is happening in today's market. By running them from time to time, investors can find trends and interesting tidbits of information on companies. Simple screens, such as the daily highest percentage gainers and losers, and which stocks had the highest volume, are put in daily newspapers every day. Screens can also show which sectors and investment styles are working or not working in the current investment environment.

SEVEN STEPS IN THE SCREENING PROCESS

The screening process can be broken down into seven steps, as shown in Figure 2-1. We will discuss each step below.

1. Determine Your Investment Theme

Investors should devise a strategy that they believe will perform well in the future. They should know what the primary factors of consideration are for their investments and rank them accordingly. They should factor in their stage of life and also their risk tolerance and return requirements. They should have a fairly clear sense of what qualities they want in their stocks. Growth? Value? High profit margins? REITs? Small cap? Low debt? For example, high-quality stocks with high dividends could be a theme.

2. Determine the Variables and Range

Investors must determine what variables need to be screened to get the characteristics they're looking for in an investment. It is important that the screener has a wide range of filters that can be chosen. The overall universe of stocks to be screened needs to be determined. All exchange-listed companies? Companies with market capitalizations above $1 billion? Companies in a specific index? In the case of an investor looking for high-quality and dividend-paying stocks, dividend yield would almost certainly be one of the factors. For the quality component, an investor may consider companies with high credit rating or those that have a long history of strong earnings numbers. Five or six variables are generally more than enough to get a viable screen.

FIGURE 2-1   Steps in the screening process.

1. Determine the theme or characteristics one is looking for in investments

2. Determine the variables and the range of variables to be used

3. Input data and run screen

4. Assess results

5. Qualitative overlay

6. Investment decision

7. Follow up, running same screen periodically

An investor should look at the financial statistics of a widespread benchmark, such as the S&P 500 or Wilshire 5000, to help determine the range to put in for their variables. For example, if the S&P 500 is yielding 1.70 percent and an investor is looking for high-dividend-yielding stocks, putting in 3 percent or higher as a range may be appropriate. An investor should also make sure that the inputs for the screen are not contradictory. For example, the Internet sector and a high dividend yield do not belong together as filters for the same screen. They mix together like oil and water.

3. Input Data and Run Screen

When inputting the data, the investor should be careful to enter the data using the specific screener's conventions. For example, when using the filter of market capitalization, some screeners represent $1 million with the number 1. On some screeners, when an individual enters the criteria for the filters, the screener lets them know how many stocks will be outputted. After the data is input into the filters, it takes just a few seconds to get the stock names that satisfy all the criteria. It is helpful if this output can be downloaded into other applications. On many screeners, an investor can specify the number of results and have them ranked in the order of how well they satisfy the screening criteria.

4. Assess Results

First, investors should double-check to make sure that the qualities the screener says the company has are true. If the screener says that the company's current ratio is 1.5 or higher, verify that it is. When possible, investors should try to run the same screen on a different screener and see if the results are similar. Ideally, a screen will give an investor between eight and 20 names. If one gets less than five or more than 25, the investor should probably adjust the inputs. The output should be a number of stocks that would be workable to do a review on. Remember, the companies that satisfied all your criteria are not necessarily the best buys. They are only as valuable as the searching criteria selected.

If an investor is not happy with the initial screening results, he or she should go back to step two and start again. Do not be discouraged, because screening is very much a trial-and-error process. If a screen yields too many stocks, their number can be reduced by either adding more filters or narrowing the range of the variables being used for the screen. If the screen yields too few stocks, widen the allowable range of variables or take away some of the filters and run the screen again.

5. Qualitative Overlay

At this stage, it is important that an investor provide a qualitative judgment to the stocks that come out as output from the screen. Depending on the monetary commitment in an investment and their own knowledge, investors should try to learn as much as they can about each of the stocks chosen. They should look up recent news stories about the company. If they have time and expertise, it is a good idea to obtain financial reports from the Security and Exchange Commission (*www.sec.gov*) and the corporation's own Web site. They should try to look at each of the company's financial statements, appropriate parts of the annual 10-ks and the quarterly 10-qs, and any analysis they can obtain from Wall Street firms.

After that, try to look at the financial statistics of the chosen companies' competitors and compare. If you do not feel comfortable doing your own analysis, have a brokerage firm or independent research company that you trust offer their opinion of the future prospects for the companies selected by the screening process. It never hurts to get a second opinion. The ultimate goal of the qualitative overlay is for investors to answer any outstanding questions they might have about the stock they're considering buying.

6. Investment Decision

This is the moment of truth for investors: They have to decide whether to purchase the stock or not. They should weigh the results from the screening process with the qualitative overlay. Investors should feel comfortable, after all, with the company they're investing in. They should know how the company earns, and how it plans to make money in the future, and go not only with their intellectual judgment, but also with their overall gut feeling before making a decision. Obviously, there is no guarantee that the stocks an investor chooses will go up in value. However, investors should feel confident that they did their homework and picked stocks that satisfied characteristics they were looking for in an investment.

7. Run the Same Screen Periodically

Just because an investment decision was made does not mean the screening process has ended. By running the same screen periodically (preferably monthly), an investor can see if the companies invested in still have the same characteristics originally screened for. Doing so may reveal a reason to possibly sell a stock, or the investor may pick up some names to consider buying. This step helps instill oversight and discipline in the screening process.

Peter Drucker, the well-known management expert, said, "Follow effective action with quiet reflection. From the quiet reflection will come even more effective action."[1] Unfortunately, most individual investors and portfolio managers focus their effort on developing candidates of suitable stocks to purchase. Then, once the stock is bought, they forget about it.

Investors should devote as much attention to a stock once they own it as they did when they were considering purchasing it. The performance of the stock purchased should be monitored. It is very important to limit the losses of bad stock selections. Investors should set a percentage level below the purchase price of a stock where they would automatically sell. A rate between 15 and 25 percent is recommended.

POINTS TO REMEMBER

► Generally, screeners do not come with instructions.

► Screeners have three parts: (1) a database of financial statistics, (2) a set of variables that you can filter, and (3) a screening engine.

► Screening removes the emotional element from security selection.

► Qualitative characteristics can never be screened for such as: the quality of a company's management, customer loyalty, and extraordinary items.

► In using the screening process, (1) determine the theme or characteristics you are looking for in your investments, (2) determine the variables to be used, (3) input data and run the screen, (4) assess the results, (5) use a qualitative overlay, (6) make an investment decision, and (7) follow up by running the same screen periodically.

---

[1] *Investors Business Daily*, December 15, 2004, A2

3

SETTING UP THE RIGHT SCREENS

An investment in knowledge always pays the best interest.

—Benjamin Franklin

ODAY, AMERICANS own stocks more than ever. More than half of U.S. households own equities, either directly or through mutual funds, up from just 20 percent in the early 1980s.

For investors to set up the appropriate stock screens, they need to understand their primary components. Financial ratios are the main ingredients. Without them, screening would not be very useful. They provide a basis to compare one company to another. In Figure 3-1, financial ratios and other financial statistics are broken down into eight categories. (Keep your thumb on this figure, to mark the page, because we will be referring to its categories throughout the chapter.)`

Many of these ratios and data points have offshoots or other ratios and data points that were not included because they convey the same theme as the financial data item provided. There are also many data items that can be screened for which

FIGURE 3-1 Screener inputs.

Universe
All Exchange-Listed Companies
Specific Index
Specific Industry
Specific Subindustry

Share Data
Price
Average Volume
Market Cap
Dividend Yield
Short Interest Ratio
Odd Lot Transactions
Shares Outstanding

Stock Performance
YTD Return
1-Month Return
3-Month Return
1-Year Return
5-Year Return
Relative Strength
Beta
Standard Deviation

Sales and Profitability
Sales Revenue
Profit Margins
ROE
ROA

Liquidity Ratios
Current Ratio
Debt/Equity
Debt/Capital
Long-Term Debt/Cash Flow
Cash/Total Assets
Dividend Payout Ratio

Valuation Ratios
Price/Earnings
Price/Sales
Price/Book
Price/Cash Flow
PEG

Growth Rates
1-Year EPS Growth
5-Year EPS Growth
Dividend Growth Rate

Miscellaneous
Debt Rating
Institutional Ownership
Average Brokerage Firms Rating
Independent Research Firms Rating
Analyst Coverage
Insider % Ownership
Technical Rating
EPS Surprises

do not add significant value to the process of finding potentially outperforming stocks. For example, on some sites there are filters such as the
number of employees a company has or which of the major exchanges
the stock trades. These do not help to determine if a stock is a worthy candidate for investment.

There is no single financial ratio or statistic that, when used alone,
will give an investor a great chance of outperforming the market. When
only one financial measure is used for a screen, the output is likely to be
stocks concentrated in one industry. No financial measure is perfect; each
has its faults. The goal of screening is to combine financial ratios and statistics in a way that mitigates the weaknesses of the individual factors and
combines them to form a quality list of potential investments.

The number of screens that can be created is infinite. Figure 3-1
includes ratios and data items that could be beneficial in the screening
process for investors looking for winning stocks. It is possible that some
of the criteria included have characteristics that could appear in more that
one category. For simplicity's sake, each ratio or data point was assigned
to one category.

It is important for an investor to know what effect adding a specific
filter will have on the results shown at the end of the screening process.
Investors should understand what type of company is likely to be
returned by applying a range of high or low values to a specific financial
ratio. But it's not necessary to apply a value for every single component
of a given screen. Many can be left blank. To create an effective stock
screen, there does not need to be more than six filters filled in. One can
get useful results with values placed in just four filters.

We'll go into the eight categories of Figure 3-1 in detail.

UNIVERSE

The Universe category (column 1 of the top section of Figure 3-1) is the
first one an investor should select. The screener needs to determine the
initial grouping of stocks to be screened. The choices in this category are
usually all listed companies, and all the companies in a specific index,
industry, or subindustry. The All Exchange-Listed Companies filter is the
broadest one available. It will pick up every common stock that is traded
on the U.S. exchanges. It will also include any American Depository
Receipts (ADRs) traded in the United States.

The Specific Index is another common filter. This is less inclusive than all listed equities. Investors should understand what criteria a company needs to be included in an index. Capitalization size, investment style, and industry sectors are the main characteristics from which an index is created. Two common indexes used are the S&P 500 and the Wilshire 5000.

The Specific Industry and Specific Subindustry classifications narrow the universe even further. Investors sometimes like to focus on companies in a specific type of business. "Consumer Discretionary" is an example of an industry, while "specialty retail" is an example of a subindustry. Morgan Stanley and Standard & Poor's developed the Global Industry Classification Standard (GICS), and Dow Jones offers a service that breaks out companies into specific industry classifications.

In certain industries some financial measures are more likely to be stressed. For instance, the dividend yield value is more important in looking at utilities and real estate investment trusts than it is for information technology companies. Investors should be aware that a company's classification can change over time.

SHARE DATA

The Share Data category (column 2 of the top section of Figure 3-1) has filters that are concerned with the characteristics of the listing of the stock on an exchange. Many stock price statistics that can be picked up in the stock page of the business section in your daily newspaper will show up in this category.

The Price filter screens stocks by their current market selling price. Some investors will not buy a stock that is below a specific price because of the volatility and the concern that the company's stock might become worthless. The majority of the stocks in the daily highest percentage gainers and losers category are stocks that sell for less than $10 a share. A lot of portfolio managers target the $5 or $10 mark as the price point below which they will not purchase a stock. Very low-priced stocks have a larger percentage spread between the bid and the offering price, and some have been targets of fraud and stock manipulation in the past. Historically, the majority of stocks that trade under $5 went or will go into bankruptcy.

Average Volume looks at, on average, how many shares change hands over a recent period, such as three months. Volume is looked at to determine the liquidity of a potential investment. The higher the average volume, the easier it is for an investor to get into and out of the stock, and also the spread between the bid and ask price is likely to be lower. Many professional money managers want stocks in their portfolios that have an average trading volume of at least 100,000 shares per day. It is imperative for them to make sure that there is an active market for a stock, so that if they put in a buy or sell order for a large number of shares, they will get a reasonable price for them.

Technical analysts look at volume to help determine a trend in a stock's performance. They believe it is a much better sign for a stock to be moving up with high volume levels than with a low amount of shares trading hands. For technicians, declines in prices with low volumes are not as bad as declines with high volumes.

Another share data item is Market Cap (for "market capitalization"), which is defined as the amount of shares outstanding multiplied by the stock's price. The market capitalization is looked at as the value of the company. Potential acquirers who want to purchase a public corporation generally have to pay a premium to this value.

Investors usually classify a market cap of below $1 billion as *small cap*, between $1 and $5 billion as *mid cap,* and over $5 billion as *large cap.* Over time, these breakpoints can change. The research departments of the large Wall Street firms pay most of their attention to large cap stocks since they earn most of their profits on these companies, through activities such as trading, underwriting their securities, and merger and acquisition deals.

Large caps are often widely represented in the daily highest volume traded stock lists. Large cap stocks tend to have strong competitive positions in their industry and a long earnings history. They can generally reap the advantages of economies of scale, reducing per unit costs by producing in large volume. Most are household names, such as General Electric, Johnson & Johnson, and Microsoft, and have a significant portion of their sales coming from overseas.

Companies with smaller market caps tend to be more volatile. With the smaller size, they can usually adjust to changes in the marketplace quicker than their larger cap counterparts. On the negative side, they are generally more difficult to liquidate and trade, with larger spreads than large cap equities. Small cap stocks are covered by fewer analysts, and subsequently there is less information available on them. Compared to large cap stocks when the U.S. economy is struggling, small cap stocks are hit with a double whammy: It is harder for them to get short-term financing from banks, and they usually have less exposure to international markets that may be doing fine while the U.S. economy is hurting.

Another share data item that is a staple of any screener is Dividend Yield. This measures the dividend paid by the company divided by its stock price. Utilities and REITs tend to be high dividend payers, while information technology and biotechnology firms usually pay out little or no dividends. For many investors looking for income from their equities, a stable and high dividend yield is important. For the most part, stocks with above average dividend yields are less volatile than those with below average yields. The dividend provides a bit of a cushion to the return when there is a price decline.

Shares Outstanding refers to the amount of shares that have been issued by the company. Most investors prefer companies that keep their shares outstanding at equal levels from year to year or that are buying back shares to reduce their number of shares. Many investors are turned off by companies that dilute their own stock by issuing more shares to raise money or to fund acquisition plans.

Companies that have recently bought back their shares are considered "buy" signals by many investors since they believe that an active stock-buyback plan is a sign of management's confidence in the company's prospects. It may indicate that high-level management thinks the stock price is cheap relative to the value of the business, and that buying the shares is a good way to deploy excess cash. Stock buybacks also have another positive component: By reducing the number of shares on the market, buybacks can boost a company's earnings per share and improve its valuation measures, since fewer shares get worked into the EPS calculation.

"Short interest" is the number of shares that have been sold short by investors and not yet covered. The Short Interest Ratio is calculated by dividing the short interest by the average daily volume of trading on the exchange. Contrary to the initial reaction of some potential investors, a high short interest ratio is considered bullish. It indicates potential demand for the stock by those who previously sold short and have not covered their sale. Generally, a short interest ratio close to 3.0 is considered bullish for a stock, and one close to 2.0 is considered bearish. The short interest ratio is an item that is looked at by momentum traders.

Another indicator used in a counterintuitive way is Odd Lot Transactions, which measure the percentage of orders of stocks that are less than 100 shares. Those who purchase less than 100 shares are mainly individual investors. Traders feel individual investors are less in-the-know compared to institutional investors and consider an increase in odd lot transactions a bearish sign. Any value above 25 percent of odd lot transactions would be looked at as a negative for the stock.

STOCK PERFORMANCE

Stock Performance, column 3 of the top section of Figure 3-1, looks at how the stock performed over different periods of time and measures its level of risk. Screeners show time periods as short as a week and as long as five years. Investors who focus on momentum frequently look at filters of shorter time periods in this category.

Screeners generally sort the performance data by showing it in absolute form and/or by the relative strength of a stock, which compares one stock's performance to those in the rest of the stock universe. The higher the relative strength number, the better the stock has performed compared to other stocks. If a stock has a 13-week relative strength of 80, for instance, it has performed better than 80 percent of the stock universe during the 13-week period. Many professional investors want to see that a stock has performed well compared to the whole universe of stocks over a period of time before plunging in and buying its shares.

Another filter that is used by momentum players is the current stock price as a percentage of the 52-week high or low range. Many momentum traders take long positions in equities that are close to their 52-week high. The risk to this strategy and to the method of buying stocks with strong relative strength are that they are subject to profit-taking by investors who made money in the stock. At any hint or perception of bad news, these companies will generally take a bigger short-term hit than stocks that had mediocre performance in recent periods.

Beta measures a stock's historical correlation with a proxy for the overall equity market, usually the S&P 500. It is a measure of an investment's nondiversifiable risk, and it gives an indication as to how a stock may react to moves in the overall market. The mathematical definition of beta is that it is the regression line of the percentage change of the stock compared to the percentage change of the S&P 500, and it generally works best when there is at least five years of price history.

A beta of 1.0 means that a stock has had perfect correlation with the S&P 500. A beta of 1.5 means that when the stock market has gone up 10 percent historically, the stock has appreciated 15 percent. A beta below 1.0 means that the stock is less volatile than the market as a whole. A stock with a negative beta tends to move in the opposite direction of the market. Money managers sometimes add low beta stocks to their portfolios to add diversification and reduce risks. Generally, aggressive growth portfolio managers, attempting to achieve large, outsized returns, tend to have many high beta stocks in accounts they manage.

A similar measure that is often used in conjunction with beta is *R-squared,* which gauges how much of a security's past returns can be explained by the overall stock market. If a security moved in perfect tandem with the market, its R-squared would be 1.0. If the security had absolutely no relationship to the market, its R-squared would be zero.

The Standard Deviation is a measure of the risk of owning a stock. It indicates the degree of variation in the stock's returns relative to the average return of the stock over a period of time. The higher the standard deviation, the higher the volatility and the greater the risk of the stock. Since standard deviation is an absolute measure, it is best used in comparison to another, similar security. For example, saying a stock has a standard deviation of 10 does not mean much. Saying a stock has a standard deviation of 10 while the overall stock market has a standard deviation of 5 is more meaningful. If returns are normally distributed, about two-thirds of them will occur within approximately one standard deviation of the mean.

SALES AND PROFITABILITY

Sales and Profitability (column 4 of the top section of Figure 3-1) looks at top- and bottom-line performance for companies. Sales Revenue is the sales per year for a given company. Some investors will not invest in a company if its sales revenue is not at a certain dollar level; many target $1 billion in annual sales as the minimum. An investor should be very cautious in investing in any company that has annual sales of less than $100 million. Historically, stocks that perform well have significant sales gains over time.

The Net Income figure reveals if a company is making money or losing it. Companies that continually lose money eventually go out of business. A segment of the investment public will not invest in a company that is not earning money. Unfortunately, there is no universal way that companies report earnings, which puts investors at the mercy of accounting manipulation. Earnings are generally displayed in one of three different ways: operating earnings, pro forma earnings, or EBITDA (earnings before interest, taxes, depreciation, and amortization).

Operating Earnings are calculated by taking a company's revenues minus its regular operating expenses. Operating expenses are the normal costs of running a business, such as payroll, rent, and advertising. Operating earnings are derived from GAAP (generally accepted accounting principles), and the items that are excluded are mainly nonrecurring expenses. Pro forma earnings are forward looking, and since they look into the future, there are some projections. Pro forma earnings may exclude operational expenses that occur only once or that occurred but have not yet been paid. EBITDA is in the middle of revenue (top line) and the net income (bottom line) on the income statement. It is used in many valuation metrics because it's less subject to tampering.

Profit Margins measure the percentage of profits that come from sales when expenses are deducted. Gross Margins are what a company earns after deducting all the costs of production; net margins measures what a company is earning after deducting all expenses. Looking at the net profit margin is a quick way to see if a company is profitable. A positive net profit margin means it is. High profit margins are an indication of good cost controls by a firm and/or favorable industry characteristics.

A company can have all the sales in the world, but if it's not earning a profit, it won't be in business very long. Companies in different industries tend to have different ranges of profit margins. For instance, software companies tend to have higher margins than supermarkets. This makes it important to compare a company's profit margin to those of similar companies. Those companies with higher margins than their competitors are in a much better position to cope with the ups and downs of the economic cycle. Those that have rising sales combined with rising profit margins are more likely going forward to have a rising stock price.

ROE, return on equity, is measured by dividing net income generated by the average amount of equity. It shows how profitably a company's management is deploying its retained capital. More than most other financial statistics, a stock's return on equity tends to revert to its historical mean. If the ROE is consistently high, the corporation is transferring its revenues into shareholders' wealth. An investor, though, should check that the company is not loading up on debt to accomplish this goal.

ROA, return on assets, is a similar ratio, measuring the amount of net income generated as a percentage of average total assets. ROA measures a company's operating efficiency without regard to its financial structure. Investors should be cautious about investing in companies with a return on assets of below 5 percent. When leverage is employed effectively, a company's ROE should be higher than the ROA. In both cases, the higher the ratio, the better. Return on assets and return on equity can be subject to some accounting manipulation.

LIQUIDITY RATIOS

Liquidity Ratios (column 1 of the bottom section of Figure 3-1) looks at the cash position of a company. Those with stronger liquidity ratios are more likely to be in business going forward. Those with more cash have more options on how to grow their business than those that do not, and subsequently, cash-rich companies are better able to benefit their shareholders. When the stock market and economy are improving, companies with strong cash positions, in most cases, are better able than their less flush competitors to exploit opportunities by making acquisitions or funding capital improvements. Also, when the stock market and economy turn sour, companies that have built up their cash position can usually handle the downturn better than rivals that have fewer liquid assets.

The Current Ratio is probably the most popular liquidity ratio. It is simply the current assets divided by current liabilities. Any time this ratio is below 1.0, it could mean potential problems for the company. The quick ratio (acid test ratio), a derivation of the current ratio, is a stricter measure of liquidity than the current ratio because it subtracts inventories (the least liquid component of current assets) from current assets. Inventory could include obsolete goods that may not be convertible to cash at anywhere near the value at which they are carried on the books.

Companies generally raise money by either issuing stock or borrowing and issuing debt. The main difference between these methods is when companies issue debt, they have to repay their bondholders. Investors prefer companies that have low debt levels. The higher the level of debt, the more important it is for the firm to have positive earnings and consistent cash flow.

The Debt/Equity ratio is the amount of debt divided by the sum of the common stock, capital surplus, and retained earnings. Generally, companies with low debt/equity ratios are in good financial health. A higher proportion of debt compared to equity makes earnings more volatile and increases the chance that a firm may default on its debt. A high percentage in debt also makes servicing it more expensive when interest rates are rising.

The Debt/Capital ratio shows how leveraged a company is. It divides the total debt by the total invested capital, which for the most part is shareholders equity plus long-term debt. A value for the ratio below 30 percent is generally viewed as favorable. Obviously, different industries tend to carry varying degrees of debt. Capital intensive businesses tend to carry higher levels of debt because of their large property, plant, and equipment costs.

Two other ratios in the liquidity category are Long-Term Debt/Cash Flow and Cash/Total Assets. Long-term debt/cash flow has been shown to be a predictor of bankruptcy for companies that have a high value. Cash flow is defined as net income from continued operations plus depreciation expense and deferred tax. Cash as a percentage of total assets gives an indication on how quickly a company can get cash internally if necessary.

The Dividend Payout Ratio looks at the amount of the dividend relative to the company's net income or earnings per share. The ratio gives an indication of whether the dividend the company is paying is sustainable. A relatively higher figure for the ratio is attractive to conservative investors looking for income. A high ratio, though, could stymie growth because less of a company's funds are available to invest in its core business. For most corporations, the dividend payout ratio should not exceed two-thirds of earnings. Real Estate Investment Trusts (REITs) are an exception because there are provisions in the tax law that encourages them to pay out almost all their earnings as dividends.

VALUATION RATIOS

Valuation Ratios (column 2 of the bottom section of Figure 3-1) focus on how a company's stock price compares to various financial statement items. In certain subindustries that are heavily influenced by commodity prices, such as oil drilling and gold mining, stock valuation measures do not provide much insight into whether a company is under- or overvalued. All the valuation ratios have the current stock price or a component of it as the numerator.

The most widely followed and talked-about valuation ratio is the P/E, or price/earnings ratio. The P/E ratio takes the price of the stock and divides it by the company's latest yearly earnings or its future projected earnings. Technology companies generally have high P/E ratios while financial companies tend to have low ones.

As a general rule, investors should be wary of companies that have P/E ratios of above 50 and below 5.0. A P/E over 50 will be difficult to sustain going forward. A positive price/earnings ratio below 5.0 generally means that investors are abandoning the stock and signals that there may be serious problems with the company. The P/E for a company can be negative if the company did not make money in its latest year or if it is not projected to in the coming year. Often there is a perception that companies play games with their earnings number.

The Price/Sales ratio is derived by taking the price of the stock and dividing it by sales per share. For this ratio, the lower the value (as long as it is positive), the more attractive the valuation. A stock with a price/sales ratio between zero and 1.0 should draw some attention by some value investors.

The Price/Sales ratio is an important measure because there are many companies that do not have any earnings. This measure is a way of evaluating companies that have an insignificant price/earnings ratio. It is often used to find young, fast-growing firms with strong sales whose earnings are small or that are currently losing money. This ratio is less appropriate for service companies like insurers, which do not have traditional sales.

A popular valuation ratio is the Price/Book ratio. Banking and industrial research analysts use this measure frequently to evaluate the companies they cover. This ratio is derived by taking the price of the stock divided by the theoretical dollar amount per common share that one might expect to receive from a company's tangible assets should liquidation occur (the breakup value).

Book value is usually determined by subtracting total liabilities from total assets and then dividing that by the number of shares outstanding.

The price/book ratio is used to separate growth and value styles in the S&P Barra indexes. If a stock has a price/book ratio above a certain value, it is considered a growth stock, and if it is below, it is considered a value stock.

This ratio is also helpful in comparing companies in different countries. Accounting standards for determining earnings vary around the world, while the definitions of assets and liabilities are more uniform. The problem with the price/book ratio is that reliable book values are difficult to determine. Assets such as plant and equipment may have substantially depreciated in value, while others such as real estate may have had a tremendous appreciation since they were recorded on the books. Furthermore, many companies have intellectual or intangible assets, such as patents, which are difficult to put a value on.

Price/Cash flow is a ratio some investors prefer over price/earnings because cash flow is less subject to accounting manipulation compared to other ratios, such as price/earnings. Cash flow is higher up on the income statement than earnings and is not concerned with assumptions that accountants make about items such as depreciation. The cash flow number backs out everything but the real cost of conducting business. It measures the amount of money that actually moved into and out of the firm's bank accounts.

Front-end income loading and deferral of costs can influence a company's reported earnings. Companies have been known to recognize sales that have technically not yet closed. Others have hidden expenses, sometimes by treating them as capital investments. This spreads out their effects on the financial statements over many years, rather than taking a onetime hit. The end result being reported earnings that are massaged to be more in line with analyst and investor expectations. These are some of the reasons that many prefer cash flow over earnings as a financial measure.

Cash flow can have many different definitions. If this ratio is used, the investor should check to see how cash flow is being defined. One definition of cash flow is net income from continued operations plus depreciation expense and deferred tax. By insisting on a positive cash flow, an investor significantly reduces the chances of picking a dog in terms of financial health.

The PEG ratio is a valuation ratio that has become more widely used in recent years. It is a terrific ratio for investors who employ the "growth at a reasonable price style" mode of investing. Overall, this is one of the best ratios to utilize in the screening process because it combines both growth and value characteristics. The PEG allows an investor to quickly see if a stock is attractively priced. Its components are three of the most important characteristics of determining whether a stock should be purchased: price, earnings, and the growth of the earnings.

This ratio is calculated by taking the current or forward price earnings of a stock divided by its actual or future earnings growth rate. A stock with a PEG ratio below 1.0 appears on the surface to be attractively valued. It suggests that investors are putting a lower price on the company's stock than they should based on its growth prospects. PEG ratio values vary widely by industry, so comparing similar companies is wise. If possible, it is also smart to try to ascertain what the historical PEG ratio has been for the company to see how the current PEG compares.

GROWTH RATES

Growth rates (column 3 of the bottom section of Figure 3-1) focuses on financial measures that have been increasing or are projected to go up in the future. The long-term value of a stock is the discounted cash flow of the future earnings stream. Growth rates of certain financial metrics are helpful in determining whether a company is undervalued or overvalued.

The 1-Year and 5-Year EPS Growth (earnings per share growth) looks at how much earnings per share have grown over those periods. *Sales growth* measures the growth in revenue for a company over a particular time period. On many screeners, EPS growth and sales growth can be evaluated on a quarter-to-quarter and year-ago quarter-to-quarter basis. The problem with these ratios is that just because a company increased earnings per share or sales in the past, there is no guarantee that it will do so in the future.

The Dividend Growth Rate measures the percentage that a company has historically increased its dividend. But again, as with earnings per share and sales, just because a company has raised its dividends in the past does not mean it will do so in the future. This ratio is useful because dividends are "sticky"—companies do not like to cut the dividend unless they have to. The reason is, when companies announce a dividend cut or announce that they're going to discontinue the dividend, their stock price generally gets pummeled.

Forward sales and *forward EPS growth rates* look at how sales and earnings are forecasted to grow in the future. It's important to know how many analysts are contributing to these forecasts, as well as the range of their opinions. If only one analyst has a forward sales forecast for a company, the number should be taken with caution. It is much better to have at least three analysts who submit forward sales and earnings growth numbers.

The *company/industry growth ratio* and *company/S&P 500 growth ratio* are important measures for determining the growth potential for a company compared to companies in their industry or companies in the overall stock universe. The company/industry growth ratio is calculated by dividing the company-to-industry five-year growth rate by the company-to-industry projected price-to-earnings ratio for the current year. The company/S&P growth ratio is derived by dividing the company-to-S&P 500 five-year projected earnings ratio by the company-to-S&P 500 projected P/E for the next year. These ratios enable an investor to see how a company stacks up compared to other similar companies and to the broad spectrum of listed companies. A higher number is a better result for both ratios.

MISCELLANEOUS

The items in Miscellaneous (the last column of the bottom section of Figure 3-1) encompass financial ratios and statistics that do not fit neatly in the other seven categories. Most of the items in this category would be classified as secondary factors to consider in screening for possible investments.

For example, Analyst Coverage looks at how many analysts are covering a specific company using fundamental analysis. It is an indication of how closely watched the company is by the research community. The more analysts covering a stock, the less the likelihood of earnings surprises. For any ratio where there is consensus outside analyst forecasts going in as an input to the ratio, it is recommended that at least three analysts provided estimates. If only one analyst is covering a stock, it gives too much weight to that analyst's forecast. In the current environment, analyst coverage is becoming more of a concern, with brokerage firms cutting down on their research staffs, and subsequently the number of firms they can cover.

Institutional Ownership looks at what percentage of the shares outstanding is owned by large institutions—namely banks, trusts, pension funds, insurance companies, and mutual funds. Investors like to see that big institutions have given their blessing by investing in the company. Market perception is that large institutional owners are smarter about investing than small individual owners. Institutions trade in much larger sums of money than individual investors. This gives them better access to the companies they are investing in and to Wall Street research.

Insider % Ownership delves into the percentage of shares owned by high-ranking officials within the company. The Securities Act of 1934 defines an insider as an officer or director of a public company or an individual or an entity owning 10 percent or more of any class of a company's shares. Corporations with a high percentage of shares owned by insiders tend to be more shareholder friendly. As a guide to what the future prospects for the firm are, investors sometimes follow if insiders are buying or selling the company's shares.

Insiders are looked at as having the most knowledge of the inner workings of the company, so if they're buying shares on the open market, it is considered a good sign for the company. Logically, insiders would not buy their company's stock if they thought it was going to decline in price. One recent academic study found that between 1992 and 1998 insiders beat the broad market by 5 percentage points per year, while typical households underperformed by 1 percent. For what it is worth, the same study found that U.S. senators outperformed the market by 12 percent per year.[1]

It makes a certain amount of sense. After all, who would be in a better position to judge a company's future prospects than its top brass? If insiders are buying the stock, it may mean management is bullish about the company's prospects. Conversely, if insiders are doing more selling than buying, it may indicate that they believe the outlook isn't all that rosy. Of course, some insider selling may be dictated more by an individual's financial needs than any desire to bail out of the stock. Investors, though, should be cautious if a large contingency of insiders is selling large positions of the stock. After all, if they thought that the prospects for the stock were incredible, you likely would not see a mass exodus by the firm's insiders.

[1] *Smart Money*, October 5, 2004

Also in the Miscellaneous category is Debt Rating. Standard & Poor's and Moody's offer debt ratings for most companies that issue debt. This rating is the opinion of how likely it is that a company can satisfy its credit obligations. The rating helps determine the interest rate at which companies are able to borrow. It should not be misconstrued as being a buy or sell recommendation.

As opposed to equity analysis, which is mainly concerned with the income statement, debt rating analysis focuses primarily on the balance sheet. Trends in the credit rating of a firm can provide an indication of what might happen to its stock price in the near future. Companies whose bonds have credit ratings in junk status (below investment grade) are viewed as very speculative in terms of their ability to repay their bondholders. There can be a big significant move in a stock if its credit rating is changed from investment grade to junk status or vice versa. It's rare to see a company having a series of credit downgrades coinciding with a large appreciation in its stock price.

EPS Surprises are the differences between consensus analyst estimates and the reported earnings. EPS surprises have been followed more closely by market players in recent years. Positive earnings surprises can be a big catalyst in sharp price-appreciation moves. Investors should try to do their due diligence into why the company had a surprise. A positive earnings surprise caused by the company guiding the analyst community with earnings numbers that were easy to beat should be looked at differently by investors than the numbers of a company that had a huge pickup in demand for its products.

The Average Brokerage Firms Rating, an average rating of a stock by outside analysts, can provide a qualitative aspect to a screen. An investor may not want to buy a security if the consensus opinion of Wall Street analysts is a "sell." Outside analyst rankings incorporate qualitative features such as customer loyalty, product quality, and the strengths and weaknesses of a firm's management team, which are impossible to screen quantitatively.

Although the amount of sell recommendations has increased in the last few years, investors should be aware that there still is a strong positive bias to analyst rankings. Investors should remember that brokerage firms are in the business of buying and selling securities. When using analyst rankings as a screening factor, it may be wise to lower them a notch so that a "strong buy" is a "buy," and a "buy" is a "hold." Some screeners have filters for independent analyst ratings that are not affiliated with a brokerage firm. Using independent research firms eliminates some of the conflicts of interests and biases that brokerage analysts can have in their buy and sell recommendations. Independent firms such as Standard & Poor's do not engage in proprietary trading, investment banking, or equity sales and marketing.

There are also overall quantitative and technical scores that can be used as criteria for screens. One such example is Standard & Poor's Fair Value model. This proprietary model gives stocks a overall rank from one to five based on financial data such as the price/book ratio, corporate earnings and growth potential, return on equity, and current yield relative to the S&P 500. A Fair Value ranking of five indicates that the stock appears to be significantly undervalued and that there is the potential for powerful price appreciation.

HOW THE SCREENING VARIABLE
CORRELATES TO
OTHER VARIABLES

As indicated earlier, it is important for investors who are screening for stocks to know the meaning of the variables. Items such as "book value" and "cash flow" can be defined differently by various sources. First, investors should confirm, in the screener's glossary, what the exact definition of the data items are and how they are calculated in the database. They should understand what they are trying to accomplish with each filter that is added to a screen. Investors should avoid financial ratios that counteract each other. For example, high betas and high dividend yields do not belong together on the same screen.

While some financial measures do not belong together on the same screen, there are others that can strengthen the theme of the filters when they are combined. The overall rating that brokerage analysts assign to a stock is a useful item in a screen. But combining the average brokerage rating with the number of analysts providing coverage makes a more powerful argument with how the Wall Street research community feels about a stock. An investor should feel different if a stock has an overall sell recommendation with only one analyst providing coverage compared to a stock that has an overall sell recommendation with 10 analysts providing coverage.

The combination of sales growth and earnings growth is another strong combination that is much better than either of these items taken separately. Sales growth by itself shows top-line growth; earnings growth taken by itself shows bottom-line growth. Combining the two shows companies that certainly are worth further analysis to see if they're worthy of purchase.

Finally, the combination of dividend yield and the percentage of times the company has increased their dividend are two other measures that, when merged, can be helpful for investors looking for winning stocks. It is nice to own a stock that pays a healthy dividend. But most investors would prefer to own a stock that pays a nice size dividend and has also increased its dividend payout for 20 straight years.

Once an investor has a firm feel for the data items on the screener and knows how to apply them, he or she is ready to start screening. In the following chapters, we'll provide numerous examples of screens. The screening filters used and the stocks that were generated by each of the screens are included. All of the screens were run on Web sites with screeners that are free or provided at no cost for customers of the financial or publishing firm that provides the screener. All the screens were run using end-of-year 2004 and beginning-of-year 2005 data.

Of course, it is probable that by the time you are reading this book, some of the stocks in the screen may change. The screens that are included are ideas about ways to look for stocks based on a strategy. Readers should focus on the strategy and then run the same or similar screens and look at the stocks that are chosen. Once there is an output of individual stocks from the screen, the investor should put them through a further analysis either by themselves or by using a brokerage or independent research firm. Learning as much as possible about a stock before investing can never be harmful. Remember, screening is a first step in the investment process, not the last.

POINTS TO REMEMBER

▶ Financial ratios are the main components of screens.
▶ Financial ratios can be broken up into eight categories: (1) universe, (2) share data, (3) stock performance, (4) sales and profitability, (5) liquidity ratios, (6) value ratios, (7) growth rates, and (8) miscellaneous.

▶ There is no single financial ratio when used alone that will give an investor a great chance of outperforming the market.

▶ The goal of screening is to combine financial ratios and statistics in a way that reduces the weaknesses of the individual factors.

▶ To create a useful screen, one can use just four filters.

▶ An investor should know the meaning of the screening variables and how they correlate with other variables.

▶ Screening is a first step in the investment process, not the last.

4

SCREENING FOR GROWTH

I think you have to learn that there's a company behind every stock, and that there's only one real reason why stocks go up. Companies go from doing poorly to doing well or small companies grow to large companies.

—*Peter Lynch*

THERE ARE NUMEROUS investment disciplines in equities to utilize to try to reach your financial goals. The investment style box in Figure 4-1 is a common way to classify stocks.

GROWTH INVESTING

Investing for growth is one of the mainstay styles for long-term investors. It is mainly geared toward people who have financial goals that are at least five years away. This investment style involves looking for companies whose sales and earnings are growing faster than the market, with the goal of finding the rising stars. It looks for firms that have both top- and bottom-line growth, ideally at a consistent or predictive rate. You should know that instead of paying large dividends to their shareholders, growth companies try to use their

FIGURE 4-1   Investment style box.

	Growth	Blend	Value
Large Cap			
Mid Cap			
Small Cap			

assets and to reinvest the profits to make their businesses expand and, over time, offer substantial capital appreciation to their shareholders. Growth companies are usually aggressive in pursuing profitable ventures and retain a substantial portion of their earnings for research and development.

In bull markets, growth stocks generally outperform value stocks. Growth stocks are highly weighted in certain sectors because certain industries tend to grow much faster than the overall economy. In recent years, most information technology and biotechnology stocks were classified as growth. Very few utility and real estate investment trusts would have been classified as such. Some current examples of growth stocks are Qualcomm (QCOM), eBay (EBAY), and Amgen (AMGN). Investors should be cognizant that over time, the sectors heavily weighted in the growth and value styles change. In another era, for example, steel and railroad companies were considered the growth stocks.

GROWTH RATIOS

Note the main ratios that money managers have historically looked at in considering whether a stock is a growth stock:

- Forward and historical Price/Earnings ratio
- Price/Sales ratio

- Price/Book ratio
- Price/Cash flow ratio

For each of these ratios, a growth stock should have valuations above the market. In general, investors are willing to pay for reliable growth. A growth stock should also have sales and earnings growth that are clearly outpacing the market's average. An investor should try to determine if the growth is sustainable and avoid issues that have achieved growth by one-time, extraordinary, or short-lived methods.

GROWTH CURVES

In general, companies stay in the growth category for a shorter amount of time than the value category. All things being equal, if you run both growth and value screens periodically, the growth screens will tend to have more turnover. For businesses, the rapid growth phase is a much shorter period of time than the mature and decline phase.

Unfortunately, trees do not grow to the sky, just as growth does not last forever. There is a limit to the amount a company can increase sales and earnings. Expansion plans have their limits. Patents and copyrights eventually expire. Product life cycles are short.

And then there's competition. If a company has tremendous earnings and sales gains, competition is likely to follow. It may be from established domestic, international, and/or start-up firms, or in a lot of cases it may come from unforeseeable places. For example, 10 years ago telephone companies didn't view cable companies as potential threats.

Another brake on growth is that employees responsible for the growth of the corporation may be harder to retain. And finally, there's always the threat of government regulation. Through antitrust legislation and sanctions, the government tries to eliminate monopolies and dissuade anticompetitive activity.

For the investor, growth stocks do come with some risk. Due to their higher valuations, lower dividend yields, and high betas, they tend to be more volatile and decline more in bear markets than nongrowth issues. Investors should thus be attuned to when a growth company is scheduled to release its earnings numbers. The day of the earnings release is usually a volatile one for a growth stock. They are often priced for perfection for their earnings release. When growth stocks miss their earnings estimates, they can be subject to harsh declines in value. Often, even when they meet their earnings numbers, they decline, because investors have such high expectations for them. They want favorable earnings surprises.

But any type of negative news can cause a sharp drop in a growth stock's price. Besides being priced for perfection, with little room for mistakes, in many cases the companies themselves are equally subject to rapidly changing technologies and developments. This can lead to quick success in the marketplace but also to obsolescence if the growth company is not careful. Eight-track tapes, walky-talkies, and slide rules are examples of products that were once considered innovative that became obsolete.

FACTORS TO CONSIDER WHEN SCREENING FOR GROWTH STOCKS

When screening for growth, an investor should look at traditional measures such as projected price/earnings and growth rates. The company/industry growth ratio and the company/S&P 500 growth ratio should also be used. These two ratios allow the screener to compare which companies are growing more than their industry and the overall market. The debt/equity ratio is also important to consider because growth fueled by massive borrowing is likely to be unsustainable. On the flip side, companies with strong cash flows can grow systemically for some time.

In terms of market capitalization, in looking for growth, an investor's bias for finding winning stocks should be in the small cap arena. (Small cap is defined as equities having a market capitalization between $100 million and $1 billion, so micro cap stocks are not included in this category.) Yes, small cap stocks are risky. Yes, they are less liquid than large cap issues. Yes, there are some high quality large cap growth stocks that will earn attractive returns. The chance, however, of getting gargantuan returns with large cap growth stocks is somewhat limited. Many of these stocks have had their big upward stock move already.

Once a business reaches a certain size, it takes much more effort and is far more difficult to grow earnings and revenues than when it was a smaller entity. The easy growth is over. If Pfizer (PFE) or Merck (MRK) comes out with a new wonder drug that cures AIDS, the effect it will have on their stock prices will be much less than if a small pharmaceutical firm produced the drug. Furthermore, large companies are less flexible and nimble. They tend to be more conservative and set in their ways. It's much harder to turn a cruise liner than a speedboat. The trick is to find quality small to mid cap companies that have good financial statistics, a workable business model, and a management team that is shareholder friendly.

It is much easier to grow sales and earnings over a longer period of time from a smaller base. For a larger cap company to continue its sales and earnings gains is very difficult. It is the same percentage gain to go from $1 million in sales to $2 million as it is from $1 billion to $2 billion. Eventually, businesses reach a saturation point. How much more can companies like Microsoft (MSFT) and McDonald's (MCD) grow? It's already at the point where they are practically in every computer and in every town.

QUALITATIVE GROWTH FACTORS

After getting the results from a growth screen, the investor should consider a few important qualitative factors before investing. First and foremost is to understand what the company's primary business and core competency is and feel comfortable with it as an investment. Many investment pundits say that if you cannot explain what a company does and how it will make money in the future in a couple of sentences, you should stay clear of the stock. If the stock goes down—which unfortunately sometimes happens—an investor who didn't understand what the company's business was in the first place is more likely to be unsure and have a difficult time making an informed decision about whether to hold on or bail out.

Investors should try to ascertain how the company plans to grow in the future. Here are four ways that firms grow:

- Creating new products or services
- Selling to new market segments, including internationally
- Expanding their product line, and marketing different applications of their existing products
- Through mergers and acquisitions

Knowing the method by which the company expects to grow in the future allows the investor to judge how it's doing and how likely it is that the company will accomplish this goal. It makes it easier for an investor to determine whether it is in fact a "growth" company.

An investor's preference should be for companies that are creating their own new products and services to generate their growth. This method, called "organic growth," is most likely to have the widest profit margins and the longest time frame for potential growth.

An investor's least favorite method should be companies that are growing by merging and acquiring. Here's why: First, firms generally have to pay a substantial premium to buy another company. And then, there are often assimilation issues and work culture differences between the staffs of the merged companies, and power struggles between high-level executives. An investor should also ask if the selling company thought its prospects were so good, why would it allow itself to be bought out? Do they know something that the acquirer doesn't?

The investor should try to answer some of the following questions to help determine if the growth stock that came out of the screen is a worth-while investment. All the questions raised are a derivative of the main qualitative issue a growth investor needs to try to determine: Is the growth sustainable?

- *Does the company have a unique or valuable product or service in the marketplace that is in demand*? A one-of-a-kind product in demand by the public is likely to give the firm pricing power and good growth prospects for the near term.

- *Does the company have any new products that are coming to market in the near future*? Companies with new products that are to be brought to market in the near future increase the potential for additional revenues and profits for the firm's bottom line. Historically, the truly great growth stocks have been innovators and have put many resources toward research and development. A study by the Harvard Business School found that the shares of companies with the greatest R&D spending as a percentage of sales often outperform (Standard & Poor's Outlook, July 14, 2004). Historically, the companies that spend a lot on R&D tend to be clustered in two sectors: information technology and health care, specifically the pharmaceutical and biotech groups.

- *Does the company have any valuable patents or trademarks, and what is their status*? Patents and trademarks offer companies protection from competition in the short term by making it illegal to copy their inventions. They award and give a motivation for corporations to invent. Firms that have some patents and copyrights have more pricing power and have a head start on their competitors who want to enter that particular product line.

- *Are the barriers to entry in the industry high?* Industries where it is difficult for start-up firms to survive generally make for better long-term growth prospects for the established companies. Industrial firms tend to have higher barriers to entry than service firms due to their high capital requirements. For example, it is less likely for a start-up company to be successful producing jumbo-jet airplanes than to open a small retail establishment that is economically viable.

- *Do they face little competition?* Obviously, fewer competitors in terms of number and intensity is better for a growth company. Companies that take advantage of their lack of rivals by gauging their customers will likely be faced with government intervention at some point. Less advertising is usually needed for companies that do not face heavy competition.

- *Does the company have a competitive advantage that will last over time?* To truly grow over the long term, the company needs to have something valuable that its competitors do not and that is difficult to copy. The competitive advantage can come in many forms, such as a well-known brand name, experienced management, location of the business, unique manufacturing process, tremendous customer loyalty, and a very low cost structure. Companies with a competitive advantage can generally leverage it and provide the potential for growth over the near term.

If a growth investor can answer yes to some of the questions raised in the preceding paragraphs, it should give him or her more of a reason to take the plunge and invest in the company that was the output of the screen.

EXAMPLES OF GROWTH SCREENS

For the remainder of the chapter, we'll examine examples of screens using the growth style. All of them were run in the first quarter of 2005. Readers should focus on the logic behind the screen. They should be aware that the stocks generated by the screens may change by the time they read the book.

All these screens are easy to formulate on screeners on financial Web sites that are free. Unless specified, each of the growth screens has a filter for a stock price of at least five dollars and a market capitalization of at least $100 million. This helps the investor avoid speculative stocks that can be extremely volatile and not very liquid. American Depository Receipts (ADRs) are included as results from the screens. Note that each growth screen has a different level of risk, and thus the stocks rendered by each should be further researched in different degrees. Be sure to use the screen that best suits your objectives.

Growth by Traditional Measures

The screen in Figure 4-2 seeks stocks that would be considered growth by four different metrics. Each of the stocks has to have a price/earnings ratio (based on both projected earnings for the next fiscal year and actual earnings in the most recent 12-month period), price/sales, and price/book value ratios at least 50 percent greater than similar current measures for the S&P 500 as of December 31, 2004. On that date, the S&P 500 had a forward P/E ratio of 17.47, an historical P/E of 19.86, a price/book ratio of 2.91, and a price/sales ratio of 1.53.

The screen mitigates outliers because none of the stocks can have a value below zero and above 100 for any of these traditional ratios. Since the stocks that are outputted are valued above the market, a question that potential investors may ask is: "Do they have room to move higher?" To help alleviate this concern, there is a filter on the screen that the average rating by Wall Street analysts has to be a "strong buy" or "buy" on the stock. The majority of analysts believe these stocks are likely to outperform going forward.

High Projected Growth and Returning It to Shareholders

The screen in Figure 4-3 looks at companies that have a five-year projected annual growth rate of at least 30 percent and a return of equity of at least 20. Firms that are projected to grow at a fast pace and have a history of transferring it to shareholders should see their stock price rise in the future if all things go according to plan. The projected growth rate

FIGURE 4-2   Traditional growth stocks.

*Search Criteria	Low Value	High Value
U.S. Markets		
Price of Stock	$5	
Market Cap	$100 million	
P/E Projected Nxt FY	26.21	100
P/E Ratio	29.79	100
Price/Book Ratio	4.36	100
Price/Sales Ratio	2.29	100
†Analysts Buy Hold Sell Mean		2

Output

Symbol	Company	Price of Stock	Market Cap in Millions	P/E Projected Nxt FY
ACL	Alcon Inc.	78.85	24,458	27.4
CTSH	Cognizant Technology	37.17	5,008	40.5
DRIV	Digital Riv Inc.	32.87	1,070	27.4
EBAY	Ebay Inc.	104.55	69,499	65.5
INFY	Infosys Technologies Ltd ADR	63.69	16,942	31.4
SGTL	Sigmatel Inc.	35.15	1,167	27.6
JOE	St. Joe Co	64.54	4,902	49.9
TSRA	Tessera Technologies	37.79	1,506	45.1
UTIW	UTI Worldwide Inc Ord	67.56	2,122	27.8
WIT	Wipro Ltd ADR	21.06	14,296	32.1

Symbol	P/E Ratio	Price/Book Ratio	Price/Sales Ratio	Analysts Rating Mean
ACL	30.3	12.6	6.5	1.9
CTSH	61.4	12.8	10.4	2.0
DRIV	40.5	6.4	8.7	2.0
EBAY	98.9	11.4	23.8	2.0
INFY	52.2	18.4	13.2	1.9
SGTL	31.4	7.5	8.6	1.9
JOE	58.6	10.0	5.6	2.0
TSRA	55.5	15.0	25.6	2.0
UTIW	35.9	4.7	3.0	1.5
WIT	51.4	14.8	9.1	1.9

*Screen was run on Businessweek.com Advanced Screener.
†1=Strong Buy, 2=Moderate Buy, 3=Hold, 4=Moderate Sell, 5=Strong Sell

FIGURE 4-3 High projected growth and a high return of equity.

*Search Criteria	Low Value	High Value
Price of Stock	$5	
Market Cap	$100 million	
Current ROE	20	100
Long-term Growth Consensus estimate	35	100
Number of Brokerage Ratings	2	

Output

Symbol	Company	Price of Stock	Market Cap in Millions	Current ROE	Long-term Growth Consensus Estimate	Number of Brokerage Ratings
AGU	Agrium Inc.	15.08	1992	25.96	50	4
APTM	Aptimus Inc.	25.16	148	33.45	50	3
BLTI	Biolase Technology	9.65	219	23.77	35	3
CTRP	Ctrip.Co Intl ADS	43.37	1308	21.67	37.5	6
NTES	Netease.Co Inc. ADS	49.97	1634	38.63	35	4
PMTI	Palomar Med Tec	23.99	386	33.77	35	2
SINA	Sina Corp	29.5	1489	34.9	40	4
SWN	Southwestern Energy	45.94	1665	22.19	43	12
TRAD	Tradestation Group	6.55	274	35.93	35	4
ULBI	Ultralife Batteries	17.75	254	26.42	38.75	7

*Screen run on Zacks Investment Screener.

was determined by the average of at least three analysts' forecasts. This is to prevent one person's projections from having too much influence.

Rising Sales and Profit Margins

A company that has been increasing its revenue while its gross profit margins are at a high level is a powerful combination. This leads to a perfect storm of rising top- and bottom-line growth. The stocks in this screen (Figure 4-4) have had sales gains annually for five years and a gross profit margin of at least 20 percent. The last filter applied is that the debt-to-equity ratio is 10 percent or less. This helps filter out companies that are fueling their growth by borrowing. Companies that are returned by this screen are certainly in a strong position for capital appreciation in the near future.

Undiscovered Opportunities

The screen in Figure 4-5 is for investors who like to be proactive and ahead of the crowd in discovering opportunities. These stocks have had earnings per share growth for five years of 75 percent or more per year. They have a filter to keep them smaller cap, with a market capitalization of $1 billion or less. These stocks have not yet garnered interest from the Wall Street research community, with only one analyst providing a "buy" or "sell" recommendation for each. If the earnings of these companies continue to grow like this, they will not be ignored for long.

Be aware that the stocks on this list can be highly speculative and should only be considered by very aggressive growth investors. One of the stocks returned by the screen, Orbit Intl Corp, only has a market capitalization of $28 million—an exception to our $100 million characteristic. While investing in these neglected stocks may pose increased risk, the rewards are potentially greater over the long term.

Strong Comparative Growth

The companies that are selected from the screen in Figure 4-6 are traded on U.S. markets and are growing at least one and half times as fast as their industry and two times as fast as the S&P 500. Companies in industries with higher growth rates will be more likely to come out as output for the screen. A filter of a minimum of $2 billion market cap was used

FIGURE 4-4 Rising sales and profit margins.

*Search Criteria	Low Value	High Value
Price of Stock	$5	10
Market Cap	$100 million	100
Debt/Equity Ratio		100
Gross Profit Margin	20	
5-Year Sales Growth	20	

Output

Symbol	Company	Price of Stock	Market Cap in Millions	Debt/Equity Ratio	Gross Profit Margin	5-Year Sales Growth
AKAM	Akamai Technologies Inc.	11.92	1,472	0.0	62.1	73.6
CHS	Chicos Fas Inc.	48.90	4,436	0.1	61.2	43.2
CTSH	Cognizant Technology	36.98	5,008	0.0	45.7	21.2
CREE	Cree Inc.	33.44	2,418	0.0	48.3	33.1
MATK	Martek Biosciences Corp.	47.77	1,407	0.0	37.6	81.6
PNRA	Panera Bread Co.	46.84	1,425	0.0	38.1	23.6
RIMM	Research in Motion Ltd.	77.02	13,706	0.4	45.6	34.1
SAP	SAP AG ADR Spon	41.39	51,536	0.0	63.6	23.9
SEPR	Sepracor Inc.	60.62	6,408	0.0	91.2	59.5
WBSN	Websense Inc.	49.85	1,050	0.0	93.2	37.1

FIGURE 4-5 Undiscovered opportunities.

*Search Criteria

	Low Value	High Value
Price of Stock	$5	
Market Cap		$1 billion
Annualized 5-Yr. Historical EPS Growth	75	
Number of Analyst Ratings		1

Output

Symbol	Company	Price of Stock	Market Cap in Millions	Annualized 5-Yr. Historical EPS Growth	Number of Analyst Ratings
BOO	Collegiate Pacf	12.30	124	90.65	1
LAYN	Layne Christens	17.45	220	136.40	1
MCRI	Monarch Casino	34.13	321	87.78	1
ORBT	Orbit Intl. Corp.	9.44	28	129.60	1
IRN	Rewards Networks	5.88	146	148.64	1
RCKY	Rocky Shoes & Bts	29.50	136	124.22	1
SCHN	Schnitzer Steel	30.92	932	77.15	1

*Screen run on Zacks Investment Screener.

FIGURE 4-6 Strong comparative growth.

*Search Criteria

	Low Value	High Value
Price of Stock	$5	
Market Cap	2 billion	
Company/Industry Growth	2	
Company/S&P 500 Growth Rate	1.5	

Output

Symbol	Company	Price of Stock	Market Cap in Millions	Company/Industry Growth Rate	Company/S&P 500 Growth Rate
CEPH	Cephalon Inc.	48.52	2,786	9.0	3.0
GGG	Graco Inc.	35.95	2,485	2.9	1.7
ITW	Illinois Tool Wks Inc.	91.00	26,914	3.3	1.9
KEP	Korea Electric Power Co. Sponsored ADR	13.12	16,523	2.1	3.6
T.NXY	Nexen Inc.	49.00	6,331	6.6	11.2
PBR	Petrobras Brasileiro ADR Sponsored	38.15	41,899	2.6	5.0
PHI	Phillipine Long Distance Tel Sponsored ADR	24.10	4,033	2.1	4.5
SNDK	Sandisk Corp.	24.85	3,990	2.2	3.2
SSL	Sasol Ltd. Sponsored ADR	20.37	12,449	2.2	4.1
WGR	Western Gas Res Inc.	28.54	2,111	2.2	2.7

*Screen run on Businessweek.com Advanced Screener.

54

so that very small cap stocks would be excluded. If they keep up this growth record, the stocks returned by the screen will soon be wanted by growth stock investors and will be possible takeover candidates for larger, slower growth companies.

POINTS TO REMEMBER

▶ The growth investment style is looking for companies whose sales and earnings are growing faster than the market.

▶ When screening for growth stocks, an investor should look at growth rates and the projected price-to-earnings rate.

▶ Investors should look at growth compared to a company's industry and the entire market.

▶ When screening for growth stocks, investors should favor small cap issues.

▶ Investors should try to ascertain qualitative features of a company, such as how it plans to grow in the future.

5

SCREENING FOR VALUE

To know values is to know the meaning of the market.

—*Charles Dow*

VALUE INVESTORS are looking to get more bang for their buck. To use a car analogy, if growth stocks were a car; they would want to be a Chevrolet Corvette, if they were a value stock, they would strive to be a Honda Accord. Value stocks often are considered boring, unglamorous, and are neglected by many. Most people would not be excited to own them. Value stocks do not get a lot of positive fanfare. In many cases they have been plagued with recent bad news and are out of favor. Their sales and earnings are growing at a pace slower than the overall market.

Value investors pay extremely close attention to the price component of a stock. The decision of whether the price of a stock is understated compared to its true worth is at the heart of every decision a value investor makes. They are frugal and hunting for bargains. Value investors are also considered contrarian. Going against the norm, they buy shares that are cheap even when others are pessimistic about them.

Benjamin Graham is considered the father of value investing. Graham felt it was very important that a company trade below what the firm would sell for if it put itself entirely up for sale on the open market. He felt that investors who ignore valuation concerns and overpay for their investments are operating with a zero margin of safety. The basic meaning of the margin of safety is that investors should only purchase a security when it is available at a discount to its underlying intrinsic value. Some of the components that he wanted a stock to have before investing in it were: a price/earnings ratio less than 40 percent of the average P/E over the last five years, a dividend yield greater than two-thirds of the AAA Corporate bond yield, a stock price less than two-thirds of the book value, and current assets greater than twice the value of current liabilities.

Although Graham wrote about most of his investment theories in the 1930s, his influence is still felt today, including by renowned modern investors such as Warren Buffett, who studied under Graham at Columbia University, John Neff, Sir John Templeton, and Mario Gabelli. Graham was quoted as saying in regards to value: "The individual investor should act consistently as an investor and not as a speculator. This means that he should be able to justify every purchase he makes and each price he pays by impersonal, objective reasoning that satisfies him that he is getting more than his money's worth for his purchase."

VALUE BENCHMARKS

The main benchmarks for value stocks against which money managers are judged are the S&P Barra Value Indexes and the Russell Value Indexes. In both of these indexes, a stock's price/book ratio is a major component. The Russell Value Indexes consist of companies that have low price/book ratios and low forecasted growth values. The S&P Barra Value Indexes are determined by looking at all the price/book ratios of the companies in the S&P 500. The median price/book ratio is determined so that there is an equal market capitalization above and below the median. Any stock above the median goes to the "growth" index, any equity below enters the "value" index.

FACTORS TO CONSIDER WHEN SCREENING FOR VALUE STOCKS

Value investors focus on many of the same financial statistics as growth investors. The historical and forward price/earnings, price/book value, price/sales, and price/cash flow ratios of companies are all studied by value-focused portfolio managers. But in contrast to those looking for growth, value managers look for companies that have values for these ratios *below* the S&P 500 benchmark. Investors should be aware that companies losing money will show up with price/earnings ratios that are negative and subsequently not meaningful. Strict value investors look for their stocks to be trading close to or below their book values. In certain stock environments, stocks with such low book values are difficult to find.

Value investors should also examine the debt ratios and the dividend yields of potential investments. A good value stock should have low debt levels, good cash flow, and a high credit rating. Although it may be out of favor by investors at the current time, the company needs to be on firm financial footing. This allows a firm to have more options on ways to improve its performance. Good value stocks should ideally have strong cash flows and a dividend yield above the S&P 500. The high yield provides a cushion if the stock doesn't offer capital appreciation immediately. These companies tend to return a higher proportion of their earnings directly to their shareholders instead of funneling it into operations.

In a screen, two secondary measures that a value stock may have some upside potential are strong insider buying and recent earnings per share surprises. Companies with both these qualities may give an investor one more reason for buying a value stock, based on the belief that improving prospects for the company may not yet be incorporated in the stock price.

Value stocks usually are less volatile than growth stocks and have a beta below 1.0. In bear markets they tend to hold up better than stocks with the growth style. They generally have less downside risk than growth stocks, but usually have less upside potential in bull markets. Even when a company is truly undervalued, value investors need to have patience. They should realize that it sometimes takes time for a company to trade at its true intrinsic value.

Value stocks are weighted heavily in defensive sectors. Many of the companies offer products that are price inelastic—meaning the amount demanded of a product is not sharply reduced when there is an increase in price. For example, if the price of insulin rises 50 percent, diabetics will still demand it at the same levels as before the price hike. Presently, some sectors that are weighted heavily in the value style are financials, real estate investment trusts, and utilities. Some current examples of value stocks are Goodyear Tire and Rubber (GT), Archer Daniels Midland (ADM), and Merrill Lynch (MER).

The main question that an investor must ask before putting money in a value stock are: Why is it a value stock? And: Why does the stock appear to be cheap?

Here are some reasons why a company becomes a value stock:

- It is in an out-of-favor industry.
- Analysts have low prospects for the company.
- The stock price is at low levels.
- The company is restructuring.
- The company is fighting for its survival, and its viability is in question.

There is a big difference between a company that is classified as a value stock because it's in an out-of-favor sector and missed its quarterly earnings target by a penny per share and a company that is a value stock because it is about to file for Chapter Eleven bankruptcy protection and may be delisted from the New York Stock Exchange.

In terms of capitalization, all things being equal, an investor's bias for value stocks should be to own large cap stocks. These stocks, with a market cap above $5 billion, are more likely to survive in an industry that has come on hard times. They generally have stronger financial structures, and if need be, can get additional financing easier than small caps. Comparatively, large cap stocks can better survive price wars and the tightening of profit margins. Finally, larger cap stocks usually have more diversity in their revenue streams in terms of customers and product lines. If one part of a large company is struggling, there is a chance that another segment of the corporation may be doing well to offset some of the problem areas of the business.

Smaller companies generally do not have this luxury. They usually have just a few products, and in many cases have one or two major customers that account for the bulk of their business. Furthermore, larger cap issues are more multinational. For the most part, they have much more exposure to international markets than small cap stocks. And foreign economies may be doing well when the United States is struggling.

The primary risk for value investors is that the stocks they invested in are cheap, and they deserve to be. The reason the valuations are so low is that their prospects appear to be grim. In a lot of cases, it takes time for a company to turn itself around. Investors in value stocks have to think for the long term and should not expect short-term windfalls. In addition, there is always the concern and the risk that the company will never rebound and the stock will decline and eventually become worthless.

QUALITATIVE VALUE FACTORS

After investors run a value screen, the main qualitative factors they should consider are:

- What is causing the stock to be a value stock?
- What catalyst will turn the company and/or industry around and cause the stock price to rise?

The stock could be a value stock because of the capital structure of its industry. It is difficult for old-line industries like steel and utilities to be fast growers. They usually remain slow growers for many years. Commodity based stocks could become value stocks just because the price of the commodity that they produce has gone down substantially. For example, if copper prices plunge, Phelps Dodge (PD) stock will certainly be affected. Cyclical companies whose prospects are highly correlated to the overall economy can flip-flop in the growth and value categories just because of changes in factors such as the growth or lack of growth of the economy, the level of interest rates, inflation, and the unemployment rate. Finally, a sharp drop in its stock price for whatever reason can cause a stock to go into the value category.

Remember that stocks are classified as "value" because their price is low compared to items such as their earnings and book value. If a stock suddenly drops in price without some relative change in earnings or book value, just by the market's action, it can cause the company to go into the value category.

With the list of value stocks that come out of the screen, the investor should try to determine what will jump-start the stock's performance. A new management team or reworked corporate strategy may signal that changes are coming for a company. If a new CEO with an impressive track record is hired, it would be viewed as a positive sign by the market. A corporation that decides to change part of their business strategy may also provide a boost for its future prospects. If the company has been using a plan that has not been working and the stock price has been suffering, a change in strategy may be the best bet for the future of the corporation.

It is very possible that the company just needs to ride out the inevitable dips in the economy and the business cycle. The firm may have recently posted disappointing results just because of the bad overall economic environment that it's facing. There are many corporations whose performance is highly correlated to a single economic indicator. For example, Paychex (PAYX), a payroll processor, is tied with the employment level, and Lennar (LEN), a home builder, is linked to mortgage interest rates. If certain overall economic factors improve, so will the company's prospects.

EXAMPLES OF VALUE SCREENS

The rest of the chapter is devoted to screens with the value style. As mentioned earlier, remember that the stocks chosen by the screen may not be the same by the time you are reading the book and that they were run in the first quarter of 2005. There is no guarantee that the stocks selected will increase in price or remain a value stock going forward. Investors should focus on the value screen itself, not the stocks returned by the screen. To reduce the number of speculative issues, all the screens have filters whereby the stocks must have a share price of at least five dollars and a market capitalization of at least $100 million.

Value by Traditional Measures

Similar to Figure 4-2 in the previous chapter, the screen in Figure 5-1 searches for stocks that would be considered value by four traditional measures (historical and forward price/earnings ratio, price/book value, and the price/sales ratio). All the stocks chosen have values for these ratios at least 25 percent lower than the S&P 500 on December 31, 2004. On that date, the S&P 500 had a forward price/earnings ratio of 17.47, a historical P/E of 19.86, a price/book ratio of 2.91, and a price/sales ratio of 1.53. To avoid outliers, all the ratios have positive values. To help the investor avoid stocks that are undervalued because they deserve to be, each of the stocks has to be rated either a "strong buy" or "buy" by the average rating of three or more Wall Street analysts.

FIGURE 5-1   Traditional value stocks.

*Search Criteria	Low Value	High Value
U.S. Markets		
Price of Stock	$5	
Market Cap	$100 million	
P/E Projected Nxt FY	0	8.74
P/E Ratio	0	9.93
Price/Book Ratio	0	1.46
Price/Sales Ratio	0	0.77
†Analysts Buy Hold Sell Mean	1	2

Output

Symbol	Company	Price of Stock	Market Cap in Millions	P/E Projected Nxt FY	P/E Ratio
ACE	Ace Ltd Ord	42.57	12,152	7.3	9.6
AG	Agco Corp.	20.41	1,817	9.8	12.2
CEA	China Eastn Airls LTd ADR	20.68	1,006	10.4	10.0
EON	E On AG ADR Sponsored	87.25	54,720	12.7	8.5
ING	ING Groep N V Sponsored	29.10	62,419	9.1	8.7
ORH	Odyssey Re Hldgs Corp	25.38	1,637	9.5	8.9
OCR	Omnicare Inc.	32.86	3,414	12.4	14.1
TOA	Tech Olympic USA Inc.	24.55	1,085	7.0	12.0
UAG	United Auto Group	28.13	1,317	11.6	10.0

Symbol	Company	Price/Book	Price/Sales Ratio	Analysts Rating Mean
ACE	Ace Ltd Ord	1.3	1.0	1.8
AG	Agco Corp.	1.4	0.3	1.9
CEA	China Eastn Airls LTd ADR	1.2	0.5	1.0
EON	E On AG ADR Sponsored	1.2	1.0	1.5
ING	ING Groep N V Sponsored	1.8	0.7	1.8
ORH	Odyssey Re Hldgs Corp	1.2	0.7	1.8
OCR	Omnicare Inc.	1.8	0.9	1.7
TOA	Tech Olympic USA Inc.	1.8	0.6	2.0
UAG	United Auto Group	1.3	0.1	1.8

*Screen was run on Businessweek.com Advanced Screener
†1=Strong Buy, 2=Moderate Buy, 3=Hold, 4=Moderate Sell, 5=Strong Sell

Smart and Safe Large Cap Value Equities

The screen in Figure 5-2 looks at value stocks that appear to be somewhat safe and held by large institutions. Each of the stocks has a historical price/earnings ratio that is above zero and at a 25 percent discount to the S&P 500. The historical P/E of the S&P 500 on December 31, 2004, was

FIGURE 5-2 Safe large cap value stocks.

*Search Criteria	Low Value	High Value
U.S. Markets		
Price of Stock	$5	
Market Cap	$5 billion	
% Held by Institutions	50%	
P/E Ratio(Trailing 12 months)	0	14.9
Dividend Yield	4%	

Output

Symbol	Company	Price of Stock	Market Cap in Millions	% Held by Institutions	Trailing 12 months P/E Ratio	Dividend Yield
MO	Altria Group	61.63	126,500	69.66	13.09	4.74
AEP	Amer Elec Pwr	33.62	13,302	64.22	13.95	4.16
BXP	Boston Pptys	59.23	6,465	87.36	14.24	4.39
BMY	Bristol Myrs Sq	24.66	47,979	65.75	14.77	4.54
EOP	Equity Office Prpt	28.17	11,359	75.89	10.51	7.10
GGP	Genl Grwth Ppty	32.74	7,160	80.22	12.50	4.40
GM	General Motors	38.39	21,684	76.69	5.60	5.21
MMC	Marsh & McLennan	30.90	16,282	74.50	10.44	4.40
MRK	Merck & Co.	31.08	68,923	58.46	11.34	4.89
NI	Nisource Inc.	22.59	5,954	71.66	14.39	4.07
PGN	Progress Energy	43.71	10,798	60.19	13.41	5.40
PEG	Public Sv Entrp	50.17	11,930	53.75	14.89	4.39
SPG	Simon Property	60.42	12,576	87.97	14.15	4.30
WM	Washington Mutual Inc.	41.03	35,576	71.93	13.07	4.39
XEL	Xcel Energy	17.70	7,086	53.13	13.61	4.69

*Screen based run on and based on data from Zacks.

19.86. The stocks offer some safety in having a dividend yield of at least 4 percent and a minimum market capitalization of $5 billion. Finally, each of the stocks has institutional ownership of at least 50 percent. Institutional owners are seen by market participants as being more knowledgeable than individual investors. If any of these stocks had a sharp decline in price at these levels, it would be seen as a surprise by the market.

Value Stocks with Strong Financials

This screen in Figure 5-3 looks for large and mid cap value stocks (market capitalization above $1 billion) that are in a strong financial position. All the companies must have a price/cash flow ratio at a discount to the market. As stated numerous times, compared to earnings numbers, cash flow is less likely to be subject to accounting manipulation. Cash is cash. The companies in this screen have a price/cash flow ratio of 10 or less. To strengthen the claim of a solid financial position, the company needs to have a current ratio of at least 2.2. Finally, all the companies have an S&P Fair Value ranking of 5. This is the highest ranking that Standard & Poor's proprietary quantitative model gives to companies that appear to be reasonably valued based on ratios such as price/book, return on equity, corporate earnings, growth potential, and dividend yield compared to the S&P 500. The companies selected by this screen appear to be worth more than what the market is showing.

Returning Value to Insiders and Outsiders

The screen in Figure 5-4 is mining for value stocks that have returned money to shareholders and insiders have recently been purchasing the stock. The value component of the screen is that the stocks need to have a price/book ratio that is at least a 20 percent discount to the S&P 500 and is positive. As of December 31, 2004, the price/book ratio on the S&P 500 was 2.91 (and in this screen the high value is 2.32). The overall return on equity for the companies needs to be at least 25 percent, which shows that these firms have been trying to reward stockholders. Finally, company insiders have been recently purchasing the stock, signaling that they may believe it is attractively priced. Stocks that satisfy these three main filters might be poised for price appreciation in the near future.

FIGURE 5-3 Value stocks with strong financials.

*Search Criteria

Search Criteria	Low Value	High Value
U.S. Markets		
Price of Stock	$10	10
Market Cap	$1 billion	
Price/Cash Flow Ratio	0	5
Current Ratio	2.2	
S&P Fair Value Ranking	5	

Output

Symbol	Company	Price of Stock	Market Cap in Millions	Price/Cash Flow Ratio	Current Ratio	S&P Fair Value
BGG	Briggs & Stratton	38.71	1,995	9.8	2.5	5
DLM	Del Monte Foods	11.17	2,355	9.5	2.2	5
FBN	Furniture Brands Intl.	23.62	1,254	9.3	4.2	5
IMN	Imation Corp.	31.69	1,078	10.0	3.6	5
MU	Micron Technology	11.17	6,841	5.0	2.4	5
NTY	NBTY Inc.	22.28	1,494	8.9	2.7	5
SFD	Smithfield Foods	28.39	3,151	7.6	2.3	5
UTSI	UT Starcom, Inc.	16.81	1,921	8.0	2.2	5
VSH	Vishay Intertechnology	13.03	1,973	7.7	3.2	5
ZLC	Zale Corp.	26.69	1,366	8.4	2.2	5

*Screen was run on advisorinsight.com.

FIGURE 5-4 Value stocks purchased by insiders.

*Search Criteria	Low Value	High Value
U.S. Markets		
Price of Stock	$5	
Market Cap	$100 million	
Price/Book Ratio	0	2.32
ROE	25	100
Insider Purchases	High	

Output

Symbol	Company	Price of Stock	Market Cap in Millions	Price/Book Ratio	ROE	Insider Purchases
CSKKY	CSK Corp Sponsored ADR	47.00	3,515	2.3	37.2	High
FRE	Federal Home Ln Mtg Corp.	69.71	48,276	1.5	45.9	High
GNA	Gerdau Ameristeel Corp.	6.10	1,351	1.5	41.8	High
IMH	Impac Mtg Hldgs Inc.	21.64	1,522	1.9	32.7	High
IRE	Ireland Bk Sponsored ADR	63.55	24,762	2.2	25.2	High
LVS	Las Vegas Sands Corp.	42.85	14,900	1.9	82.5	High
LPL	LG Philips Lcd Co Ltd Spons ADR	19.45	11,779	2.0	58.7	High
PBR	Petrobras Brasileiro ADR Sponsored	39.05	42,414	2.1	30.4	High
PCU	Southern Peru Copper Corp	44.48	3,510	2.3	27.4	High
VHI	Valhi Inc.	15.63	1,882	2.0	38.4	High

*Screen was run on BusinessWeek Online Advanced Screener.

Highly Rated Low Price/Sales Stocks

The screen in Figure 5-5 looks at large cap equities (stocks with a market cap of at least $5 billion) that have the value characteristic of a low price/sales ratio. This is important because many companies do not have earnings and consequently the price/earnings ratio is irrelevant. This ratio is a way to put a comparative valuation on a wider scope of firms. To be selected by the screen, a stock has to have a price/sales ratio below 1.15, which is 75 percent of the S&P 500 value as of December 31, 2004. Another filter for the screen is that the company recently had an average positive earnings surprise of at least 25 percent over the past four quarters.

Companies that report recent positive earnings surprises tend to out-perform the overall market, but a positive earnings surprise can still mean that the company is not earning money. A stock that was predicted to lose 10 cents a share but reports losing only five cents a share will be picked up as a positive earnings surprise.

Finally, the current average brokerage recommendation for the stocks needs to be a "buy" or a "strong buy" with a minimum of three analysts providing their opinion on the security. Investors searching for value stocks should find an interesting group of equities returned by this screen.

POINTS TO REMEMBER

▶ Value investors pay very close attention to the price component of a stock.

▶ Value stocks trade at relative valuation levels below the overall S&P 500.

▶ Good value stocks should have low debt levels, strong cash flow, and pay a dividend.

▶ Helpful secondary measures when screening for value stocks are recent insider buying and earnings per share surprises.

▶ Large cap stocks are preferable for value stocks.

▶ Investors should try to ascertain why a company is a value stock.

▶ There is a big difference between the future potential stock per-formance of a value stock that is simply overlooked and priced cheaply, and one that is inexpensive because it will most likely be out of business in the near term.

FIGURE 5-5   Large cap value with low price/sales ratios.

*Search Criteria	Low Value	High Value
U.S. Markets		
Price of Stock	$5	
Market Cap	$1 billion	
Price/Sales	0	1.1672
Average EPS Surprise(Last 4 Quarters)	25	
†Current Brokerage Recommendation	1	2
Number of Broker Ratings	3	

Output

Symbol	Company	Price of Stock	Market Cap in Millions	Price/Sales Ratio
AG	Agco Corp.	20.57	1,857	0.39
ACGL	Arch Cap Gp Ltd	37.47	1,303	0.43
RE	Everest Re Ltd	87.39	4,905	1.01
ORH	Odyssey Re Hldg	25.34	1,641	0.65
OSK	Oshkosh Truck	65.01	2,305	1.02
PPC	Pilgrims Prid-B	32.70	2,177	0.41
PTP	Platinum Undrwt	29.46	1,267	0.93
SCS	Steelcase Inc.	12.83	1,902	0.77
UGI	UGI Corp.	38.85	1,990	0.53
UDI	UTD Defense Ind	44.59	2,262	1.02
WGII	Washington Grp	39.88	1,016	0.37
WCI	WCI Communities	28.65	1,278	0.78

Symbol	Average EPS Surprise (Last 4 Quarters)	Current Brokerage Recommendation	Number of Broker Ratings
AG	40.09	1.94	9
ACGL	51.96	1.78	9
RE	37.94	2.00	11
ORH	25.26	1.50	4
OSK	25.92	1.75	4
PPC	43.44	2.00	6
PTP	25.40	1.78	9
SCS	149.82	1.67	3
UGI	396.09	2.00	4
UDI	26.05	2.00	10
WGII	305.54	1.00	3
WCI	33.96	1.75	4

*Screen was run on Zacks Screener.
†1 = strong buy and 2 = buy.

6

C H A P T E R

SCREENING FOR GROWTH AT A REASONABLE PRICE

> Never overpay for a stock. More money is lost than in any other way by projecting above-average growth and paying an extra multiple for it.
>
> —*Charles Neuhauser (Bear Stearns)*

CREENING ALLOWS investors to search for stocks in all the major investment styles. The Growth at a Reasonable Price (GARP) investment style is a hybrid methodology. It combines the key attributes of both the "growth" and "value" styles. GARP reduces the main weaknesses and accentuates the positives of each of these styles. Peter Lynch, the legendary former portfolio manager of the Fidelity Magellan Fund, was a big proponent of GARP. During his tenure as portfolio manager, the mutual fund returned 29 percent on average, annually, results that certainly would garner interest in any investment style that was followed.

The main weakness of the growth style alone is that it pays little attention to the price one is paying for the stock. The thinking goes: As long as the revenue and earnings are

71

growing, the stock price will rise to reflect it. When the growth slows, these stocks can be subject to sharp declines.

The main fault with the value style is that many of the companies considered "value" are cheap because their prospects going forward are poor. There is no bargain in buying a stock that is inexpensive. A decision to buy should be based on its fundamentals.

The GARP style tries to solve the problems inherent in these two approaches by selecting stocks that are growing but are priced at attractive levels. Even if a company has a high price/earnings ratio, if its annual earnings are projected to grow at a higher rate than the P/E, its stock would appear attractively priced.

Like growth investors, GARP investors want companies whose sales and earnings are rising. They just want to be reasonably sure they are not getting caught up in a frenzy and overpaying for that growth. This happened in the late 1990s when investors were willing to pay inflated prices for Internet stocks such as Amazon.com and Priceline.com whose forecasted growth rates were exorbitant despite having no earnings. As fast as many of these stocks went up, they came crashing down even faster when it became evident they could would not come close to reaching their revenue and earnings targets. GARP investors aim to avoid buying overinflated stocks because, like value investors, the price paid for the growth is a strong consideration in determining whether a stock is worth purchasing.

The GARP discipline, therefore, cuts two ways. It prevents analysts and portfolio managers from recommending growth stocks trading at unreasonable prices as well as value plays with no growth prospects. In other words, GARP-based analysts are trained to look for growth and to be price sensitive.

Standard & Poor's and many others believe GARP has served investors well over long periods of time because: (1) It is an investment discipline that is not subject to market "drift" (such as growth versus value; large cap versus small cap, etc.) and (2) the discipline of selecting stocks with growth characteristics only if they trade at reasonable price levels prevents portfolio managers from succumbing to chasing near-term trends in the markets only to be victimized when the next trend suddenly emerges.

Growth at a Reasonable Price is the main style S&P analysts use in evaluating stocks. Since 1987, Standard & Poor's has categorized equities within five rankings. Five stars (strong buy) are the highest ranking. These are stocks whose total return S&P believes will outperform the total return of the S&P 500 Index by a wide margin over the next six to 12 months, with shares rising on an absolute basis. One-star stocks (strong sell) are the lowest ranking. Their total return is expected to underperform the total return of the S&P 500 Index by a wide margin, with shares falling in price on an absolute basis. Three-star stocks are considered a "hold" by Standard & Poor's equity analysts. Their total return is expected to closely approximate that of the total return of the benchmark, with shares generally rising in price on an absolute basis.

The GARP strategy has worked well for Standard & Poor's over the long term. This is illustrated in Figure 6-1. From December 31, 1986, to December 31, 2004, the five stars have returned 16.5 percent, annualized, outpacing the S&P 500 by 7.12 percent. One stars have returned 0.42 percent, annualized, over the same period, underperforming the S&P 500 by 8.96 percent. Over the same time period, the S&P 500 had a return of 9.38 percent, annualized. Attribution analysis of S&P stars performance since inception (December 31, 1986) reveals:

- Higher growth characteristics than the S&P 500
- Relatively lower valuations than the S&P 500
- Higher risk-adjusted returns than the S&P 500
- Outperformance has been primarily due to stock selection and small stock exposure.

FACTORS TO CONSIDER WHEN SCREENING FOR GARP STOCKS

The single best ratio for screening for GARP stocks is the PEG ratio. This measure is calculated by dividing a stock's price/earnings ratio by its growth rate. If a company has a forward P/E ratio of 40 and Wall Street expects the earnings to grow 30 percent annually, the PEG ratio for this company would be 1.33 (40 divided by 30). GARP investors generally are looking for stocks with a PEG ratio above zero and below 1.0, where a company's growth rate is greater than its P/E ratio. The goal is to try to select stocks with demonstrated earnings growth before the market realizes the company's full potential and bids up the P/E ratio.

Some GARP investors prefer to use the actual earnings growth rate over the past 12 months; it is preferable to use the forecasted growth rate, provided there are at least three analysts' estimates. If the forward PEG is higher than the trailing PEG, the market may expect growth to slow

FIGURE 6-1   Standard & Poor's performance ratings.

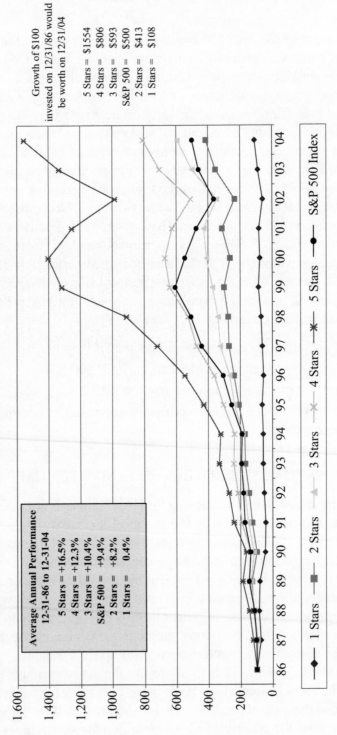

Average Annual Performance
12-31-86 to 12-31-04

5 Stars = +16.5%
4 Stars = +12.3%
3 Stars = +10.4%
S&P 500 = +9.4%
2 Stars = +8.2%
1 Stars = 0.4%

Growth of $100
invested on 12/31/86 would
be worth on 12/31/04

5 Stars = $1554
4 Stars = $806
3 Stars = $593
S&P 500 = $500
2 Stars = $413
1 Stars = $108

1 Stars   2 Stars   3 Stars   4 Stars   5 Stars   S&P 500 Index

down. On the other hand, if the forward PEG is far below the trailing PEG, the estimates may be too aggressive. Investors should try to understand why the forward and historical PEGs differ.

The PEG ratio does have some weaknesses. Like the stand-alone price/earnings ratio, it does not help in evaluating companies that are losing money. The ratio also relies heavily on analyst estimates, and their predictions for future growth rates can be wrong. Analysts' expectations of a company's future growth tend to be overly optimistic. With this knowledge of their overconfidence toward companies' forecasted growth, it is advisable that strict GARP investors should adjust the PEG ratio results they're looking for from a positive value below 1.0 to a positive value below 0.9.

Finally, PEG ratios are less useful in evaluating companies where assets are a more important determinant of value, such as in the banking and industrial sectors. Investors would need to use other ratios to determine GARP stocks in these cases.

When screening for GARP, investors are generally looking for more conservative growth numbers than the typical growth investor. GARP investors question the sustainability of extremely high growth projections and are concerned that if a company misses these high forecasts, the stock will get pummeled. Relative high gross margins lends credence to the fact that the company's growth will continue in the near term. A strong return on equity and low debt levels are seen as positives by GARP investors. A high return on equity combined with a low debt/equity ratio shows that the firm is profitable and that their high growth rates have not been achieved by the risky method of using a lot of leverage. Like all ratios, an investor should compare them with their peer group competitors as well as the market as a whole. Another growth characteristic that is seen as a plus is earnings momentum. Investors want to see a positive trend for a company's income numbers.

In terms of the value component of GARP, investors are looking for valuation ratios such as the price/earnings ratio, price/sales ratio, and the price/book ratio to be reasonable for the company, especially when compared to its peers. Using the price/book and the price/sales ratios helps reduce some of the weaknesses of the PEG ratio. The price/sales ratio allows an investor to evaluate companies that are losing money, and the price/book ratio is a good measure for firms where assets play a large role in valuation. There is no absolute number that GARP investors are looking for in these valuation ratios. It provides more of a reason for a

GARP investor to buy a stock, though, when these valuations are below other firms within their industry.

When screening for potential GARP stocks to invest in, besides finding stocks that have above average growth characteristics and are priced at inexpensive levels it is also helpful to consider some secondary measures that may provide support to the underlying financial measures and possibly act as a catalyst to make the stock appreciate. The number of analysts covering the stock is important for GARP stocks. A company's growth rate is one of the primary components a GARP investor looks at. It is a much more meaningful number when at least five analysts are contributing their growth estimates. When only two analysts or less are providing growth forecasts, the number is subject to a gigantic amount of influence from a very limited amount of sources.

Positive earnings per share surprises and/or recent insider buying may provide additional signs that things are on the upswing for the GARP stock. Positive earnings surprises indicate that the analysts underestimated the company's performance. This usually means that the stock price should follow suit and move up to support the stronger earnings number. If the stock doesn't appreciate, it would appear to be an even bigger bargain. GARP stocks that have had recent insider buying also provide fuel on the fire for someone considering them. Insiders have as good an understanding as anybody of a company's prospects going forward. Studies have shown that insiders have been able to outperform the market on their buys, but not on their sells.

QUALITATIVE GARP FACTORS

The main qualitative factors an investor should consider after running a GARP-based screen are a reflection of its hybrid nature between the growth and value styles. The two main questions an investor should have about a GARP stock are:

- Is the growth sustainable?
- Why is it inexpensively priced?

On the face of it, these stocks have the best of both worlds: growing earnings and revenues with an attractive valuation. The investor should try to decipher through his or her own analysis or through the help of a brokerage or independent research firm why the stock based on quantitative financial measures seems too good to be true. In a lot of cases there can be a catch.

In recent times, stocks of home builders, for-profit education, and energy service companies have had a large representation in the GARP universe. Each of these groups have qualitative factors that provide some tarnish to their intriguing longer-term financial valuations. In the early 2000s, home-builder stocks skyrocketed while mortgage interest rates were heading toward their lowest levels in a generation. These companies benefited from a huge demand for housing units caused by the lower mortgage rates. Home-builder's revenues and earnings were rapidly growing while their forward price/earnings ratios were in the high single digits, well below the market averages. The main reason these stocks appeared to be so cheap was that investors felt that interest rates were going to move upward, which would make home ownership less affordable and sharply reduce the demand for housing.

For-profit education stocks also benefited in the recent low job-growth recession. Many individuals sought additional training to learn new skills and to help improve their marketability for finding potential new job openings. For-profit education companies had expanding enrollments, which translated into higher sales and profits, while their multiple-to-earnings was reasonable. One of the qualitative factors that investors had to be concerned with were what would happen if the job market rapidly improved. In addition, there were accusations that some of the leading companies in the industry were falsifying student records. There was a perception that the quality of the product was severely tainted, which led many investors to stay clear of this industry.

Energy service firms have also been in the GARP category recently. With energy prices at record levels, the demand for their services has been enormous. Contributing to this demand is the fact that many places where oil is produced are not politically stable. This increases the desire to find new places to search for energy. Despite their high growth and earnings prospects, these stocks were attractively valued because the perception by the market was that energy could not remain at such lofty levels for the long term.

The examples of these subindustries that have recently had GARP characteristics reinforces the point that investors still must consider subjective factors before investing in a stock. To judge purely by financial measures, these stocks would look like no-brainer "buys." But the fact is, investors have to do some investigating after a screen returns a list of stocks.

EXAMPLES OF GARP SCREENS

The examples of screens below incorporate the GARP style. Readers should be aware that they may end up with different output if they run these screens, which were run in the first quarter of 2005. Unless specified, all of the stocks returned from a screen will be traded on U.S. markets, have a price of at least five dollars and a minimum market capitalization of $100 million. Finally, since analyst growth forecasts are imperative in searching for potential GARP stocks, all the screens also have a filter that at least three analysts provided their estimates for a company's growth rates.

Solid GARP Stocks with Low PEG Ratios

The screen on Figure 6-2 searches for stocks with market capitalizations above $1 billion and forward positive PEG ratios of 0.75 or less. These stocks have growth rates that are greater than their P/E ratios. The PEG ratio filter is set at 0.75 instead of 1.0 (which many GARP investors use) to reduce the chance of incorporating overly optimistic analyst growth forecasts. There is a filter for the companies to have a trailing 12-month earning per share number of at least zero to make sure that all the companies returned will be earning a profit. The screen also has filters for an above average return on equity ratio and a below average debt-to-equity ratio. Each of the companies needs to have a current return on equity of at least 20 and a debt/equity ratio of 5.0 or less, lending support that these companies are earning money and returning it to stockholders without having to borrow substantially. Finally, all the companies have at least five analysts covering them, and at least 50 percent of their ratings are a "buy" or a "moderate buy." Most investors would agree that the stocks returned by this screen based solely on their quantitative financial numbers look like very good candidates for a GARP investor to purchase.

GARP Stocks without the PEG Ratio

As stated earlier in the chapter, when screening for GARP stocks, the forward PEG ratio is the single best measure. The PEG ratio does have its faults, however. The screen in Figure 6-3 returns GARP stocks with-

FIGURE 6-2   Highly rated GARP stocks with low PEGs.

*Search Criteria	Low Value	High Value
U.S. Markets		
Price of Stock	$5	
Market Cap	$1 billion	
PEG Ratio	0	0.75
Current ROE	20	
Debt/Equity		5
Number of Broker Ratings	5	
†Current Brokerage Recommendation	1	2
12-Month Trailing EPS	0	

Output

Symbol	Company	Price of Stock	Market Cap in Millions	PEG Ratio	Current ROE
ATYT	ATI Technologies	18.12	4,515.47	0.73	25.02
CTX	Centex Corp	60.69	7,543.40	0.51	26.45
ELAB	Eon Labs Inc.	26.45	2,349.37	0.69	27.32
HOV	Hovnanian Entrp	51.54	3,220.32	0.34	34.73
OMM	OMI Corp.	17.10	1,464.27	0.42	25.26
PHM	Pulte Homes	65.99	8,417.35	0.54	22.06
RYL	Ryland Group	59.90	2,849.20	0.65	33.77
TOL	Toll Brothers	74.38	5,630.42	0.63	24.24
XTO	XTO Energy Inc.	34.89	9,083.05	0.67	26.05

Symbol	Debt/Equity	Number of Broker Ratings	Current Brokerage Recommendation	12-Month Trailing EPS
ATYT	0.03	21	1.90	0.9
CTX	3.34	12	2	6.53
ELAB	0.00	6	2	1.12
HOV	0.18	7	1.29	5.45
OMM	0.71	8	1.75	2.02
PHM	0.70	13	1.85	6.4
RYL	0.61	10	2	5.85
TOL	0.90	14	1.93	5.1
XTO	0.85	24	1.93	2.03

*Screen was run on Zacks Screener.
†1-strong buy and 2-buy.

out using the PEG ratio. The value components of GARP are represented by a low price/book and price/sales ratio. The filter for the price/book ratio is a positive value of 2.0 or below, and the filter for the price/sales ratio is a positive value of 1.6 or less. The growth part of the screen is represented by a better than average growth ratio. As defined by the

FIGURE 6-3   GARP stocks without PEGs.

*Search Criteria	Low Value	High Value
U.S. Markets		
Price of Stock	$5	
Market Cap	1 billion	
Growth Ratio	0.7	
Price to Book	0	2
Price to Sales	0	1.6
†Analyst Rating		3

Output

Symbol	Company	Price of Stock	Market Cap in Millions	Growth Ratio
AZ	Allianz Aktiengesellschaft SP ADR	12.40	45,702	0.70
AAUK	Anglo Amern Plc ADR	23.38	34,413	3.30
CSR	Credit Suisse Group ADR Sponsored	40.22	44,143	2.00
GM	General Motors Corp	36.59	20,972	0.80
KEP	Korea Elec Pwr Co Sponsored ADR	13.36	17,001	1.2 0
LTW	Loews Corp.	70.32	12,874	0.90
MET	Metlife Inc.	40.59	29,826	1.00
PRU	Prudential Finl Corp	54.50	27,640	1.30
SLF	Sun Life Finl Inc.	32.60	19,494	1.20

Symbol	Company	Price/ Book	Price/ Sales	Analyst Buy Sell Mean
AZ	Allianz Aktiengesellschaft SP ADR	1.20	0.40	3.0
AAUK	Anglo Amern Plc ADR	1.50	1.60	3.0
CSR	Credit Suisse Group ADR Sponsored	1.40	1.00	2.5
GM	General Motors Corp	0.80	0.10	2.9
KEP	Korea Elec Pwr Co Sponsored ADR	0.50	0.80	3.0
LTW	Loews Corp.	1.10	0.90	3.0
MET	Metlife Inc.	1.30	0.80	2.4
PRU	Prudential Finl Corp	1.30	1.00	2.3
SLF	Sun Life Finl Inc.	1.60	1.10	3.0

*Screen was run using Businessweek.com Advanced Screener.
†1=Strong Buy, 2=Moderate Buy, 3=Hold, 4=Moderate Sell, 5=Strong Sell

FIGURE 6-4   GARP stocks with positive forward PEGs.

*Search Criteria

	Low Value	High Value
U.S. Markets		
Price of Stock	$5	
Market Cap	$100 million	
PEG Ratio	0.9	
Gross Profit Margin	45	
Pos. Earnings Surprises (Last 90 Days)	40%	

Output

Symbol	Company	Price of Stock	Market Cap in Millions	PEG Ratio	Gross Profit Margin	Pos. Earnings Surprises (Last 90 Days)
APTM	Aptimus, Inc.	22.85	134	0.60	85.70	85.70
ATPG	ATP Oil & Gas Corporation	18.66	463	0.60	80.20	100.00
KOF	Coca-Cola FEMSA, S.A. (ADR)	22.95	4,200	0.90	100.00	100.00
CNCT	Connetics Corporation	22.73	809	0.50	42.90	42.90
CUTR	Cutera, Inc.	12.99	140	0.90	49.00	49.00
INSP	InfoSpace, Inc.	40.80	1,300	0.80	48.00	48.00
LCBM	Lifecore Biomedical, Inc.	15.30	198	0.70	63.60	63.60
ORCC	Online Resources Corp.	7.89	138	0.80	57.10	57.10
SRDX	SurModics, Inc.	28.08	494	0.90	47.60	47.60
UTHR	United Therapeutics Corporation	42.53	948	0.70	68.80	68.80

*Screen was run using Fidelity's Stock Screener.

Business Week screener, the growth ratio is the ratio of a company's five-year projected earnings to its projected P/E ratio for the next fiscal year. To be included in the screen, the company needs a growth ratio of 0.7 or greater. Finally, all these stocks need to have an average ranking of at least a "hold" by Wall Street firms. These stocks returned by this screen satisfy the criteria to be classified in the growth-at-a-reasonable-price category.

GARP Stocks with Wind at Their Backs

The screen in Figure 6-4 is looking for stocks with positive forward PEG ratios at 0.9 or less. The stocks also need to have a gross profit margin of 45 or more (the market median gross profit margin is 38). A company with a high gross margin generally has products with a high market share and does not spend a great deal of money producing them. Gross margin is also a number that is not easily manipulated and is therefore a fairly reliable indication of a well-run firm. Finally, the company had to have a positive earnings surprise of at least 40 percent in the last 90 days. Companies that pass these filters on the surface look like worthy candidates for further inspection.

POINTS TO REMEMBER

▶ Growth at a reasonable price combines the strengths and reduces the weaknesses of the growth and value investment styles.

▶ GARP investors try to avoid companies that are inexpensive because they deserve to be, and they try to avoid companies that are growing but are priced at extremely high valuations.

▶ The single best ratio for screening for GARP stocks is the forward PEG.

▶ GARP investors prefer the forward PEG ratio to have a value between zero and 1.0.

▶ Before investing in a particular stock a GARP investor should ask: Is the growth sustainable? And: Why is it inexpensively priced?

7

SCREENING FOR DIVIDENDS

Do you know the only thing that gives me pleasure? It's to see my dividends coming in.

—John D. Rockefeller

HERE IS A SEGMENT of the investing public looking for income from their financial assets. In a lot of these cases, retired and elderly individuals want a large portion of their assets to have some type of income component. With the graying of America and the so-called baby boomers beginning to retire, this segment of the population is set to grow significantly over the next few years.

In the stock market, investors achieve income primarily through dividends, and as a generalization, companies that offer dividends are in good financial condition. Dividend payers have to be able to set aside a portion of their capital and distribute it to their shareholders, and they tend to have strong balance sheets and consistent earnings growth.

There are only two dates an investor needs to know when it comes to dividend payments: the record date and the distribution date. The record date is when everyone who is a shareholder at the close of that business day is entitled to receive the

FIGURE 7-1　Percent of companies paying dividends.

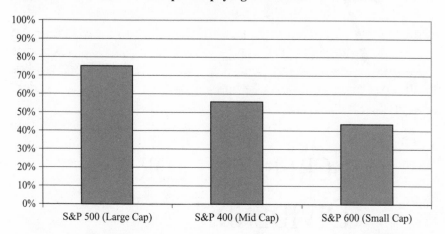

dividend. After that date, the stock is said to trade ex-dividend (meaning without the dividend). During the ex-dividend period the price of the stock is reduced by the amount of the dividend, because a new buyer of the stock will not get the current dividend. The other important date is the distribution (pay) date. This is the date when the dividend is actually paid to the stockholders. It may be a few days to a few months after the record date.

About 57 percent of companies in the S&P 1500 pay a dividend to their shareholders. The large cap S&P 500 has a higher proportion of companies paying a dividend than the small cap S&P 600 (Figure 7-1).

The overall S&P 500 currently yields approximately 1.7 percent. In terms of common stocks, sectors that currently offer high dividend yields are utilities, REITs, and financials. With that, investors should be aware that screening for very high yields as the only filter will result in a portfolio concentrated in the utilities and REITs sectors.

Many investors like the idea that in the near future they will get actual tangible money from a stock. They believe in the adage, "A bird in the hand is worth two in the bush," and often seem reluctant to sell stocks that will give them another payment within three months. On the other hand, they may be perfectly willing to sell a stock that they bought only for its appreciation potential, if that potential has not been reached. Overall, you can count on dividends being paid more than you can be certain that capital appreciation will be achieved.

You'll hear investors who are not enamored with dividend-paying stocks say that companies paying dividends have nothing better to do with the money, and that these stocks do not offer superior returns in a strong market. On the other hand, the betas on dividend-paying stocks are below that of nonpayers, meaning that these stocks are less volatile. So, while dividend payers do not usually advance as rapidly as nonpayers in a strong bull market environment, their stability in flat and bear markets tends to pay off over time. Many investors believe investing for dividend yield provides a "safe harbor" in times of uncertainty.

In fact, the returns on dividend-paying stocks have been better than nonpayers over the long term. Between 1980 and August 2004, payers in the S&P 500 have had an annualized total return of 14.86 percent, compared to 12.22 percent for nonpayers. Dividends have accounted for much more than a token portion of the long-term return on stocks. Since 1926, dividend payouts have accounted for 41 percent of the stock market's total return, according to Ibbotson Associates (*Smart Money*, May 2004). In *Stocks for the Long Run*, Jeremy Siegel details that the total nominal return from stocks between 1926 and 2001 averaged 10.2 percent per year. The components of this return were inflation of 3.1 percent , real capital appreciation of 2.7 percent, and, the largest factor, dividends of 4.1 percent .

David Dreman, a veteran value portfolio manager, did a study of dividend stocks. He divided 1,500 large U.S. stocks into five quintiles based on the size of the yield over different time periods. He found the highest yielding quintile did better than the lowest yielding quintile in each of the time periods. Results of his study are shown in Figure 7-2.

Investing in dividend stocks has received a recent boost through tax law changes that were implemented in 2003. Under the new law, capital gains and dividends are taxed at the same 15 percent rate. Before,

FIGURE 7-2   Study of dividend stocks.

*Annualized Total Returns

Compustat 1500	10 Year 1994–2003	20 Year 1984–2003	1970–2003
High Yield	13.3%	14.7%	14.5%
Average Yield	11.1%	12.6%	12.6%
Low Yield	9.1%	9.7%	8.8%
S&P 500	11.0%	12.9%	11.3%

*Data: Dreman Value Management, *Forbes* article (April 18, 2004).

dividends were taxed at a higher rate than capital gains. With capital gains and dividends now taxed on an equal playing field, this legislation has already increased the interest of yield-producing stocks for investors who have taxable investment accounts.

After the law was passed, companies of all kinds announced that they were going to review their dividend policies. According to the Cato Institute, which published a briefing on the effects of the dividend tax cut: Annual dividends paid by S&P 500 companies rose 18 percent, from $146 billion to $172 billion; 22 companies in the S&P 500 that previously did not pay dividends decided to distribute regular ones; and equity values rose more than $2 trillion from May 2003 through May 2004 (*Barrons*, November 1, 2004, 37). The new dividend tax law is set to expire at the end of 2007. If the law is not renewed by Congress, dividends will revert to being taxed as ordinary income.

FACTORS TO CONSIDER WHEN SCREENING FOR DIVIDEND STOCKS

When screening for dividend stocks, the first and most obvious place most investors look is at a firm's current dividend yield. The yield number that is widely circulated for a stock is based upon the current stock price and historical dividends. Investors generally want to see a dividend yield that is above what they could receive on a certificate of deposit (CD) or on a Treasury bill. They should also see what the yield on a popular stock benchmark like the S&P 500 or Dow Jones Industrial Average is and try to select stocks that have a higher yield.

No one should purchase a stock solely because it offers a high yield. Investors should proceed with caution when a common stock has a yield higher than 8 percent, especially in a low interest rate environment. They must determine if it is likely that the company will be able to pay out the dividend. In a lot of cases, companies that previously paid out dividends and have a sharp price decline can have seemingly high current dividend yields. This does not mean that they will automatically pay out a dividend in the future; a high dividend yield does not necessarily mean a high dividend payout.

Investors looking for dividend stocks should try to find companies with a consistent historical pattern in their dividend policy. Figure 7-3 lists stocks that have paid dividends for each of the last 100 years.

FIGURE 7-3   Stocks that have paid dividends for 100 years.

Company	Cash Dividends Paid Each Year Since
Stanley Works	1877
Consolidated Edison	1885
Lilly (Eli)	1885
Johnson Controls	1887
Procter & Gamble	1891
Coca-Cola Co.	1893
First Tennessee National	1895
General Electric	1899
PPG Industries	1899
TECO Energy	1900
Pfizer, Inc.	1901
Chubb Corp	1902
Bank of America	1903

Source: Standard & Poor's Quantitative Services

Investors should not become enamored with stocks that paid out a onetime large dividend because of some kind of special circumstances. It is important to see a company's historical dividend record. Some firms pay out the same dollar dividend amount each year, while the preference of many investors would be to look for companies that have consistently increased the dollar amount paid out year in and year out. By increasing the dividend payout each year, there is a better chance that the overall yield will increase.

Dividend-focused investors should be wary of companies that do not have a long history of paying dividends. An investor should want consistently paying dividends to be an ingrained part of the corporation's culture.

It's also important to see how its dividend policy was affected by changes in a company's performance and the overall economic climate over the years. The likelihood is high that companies paying the same dividend or that have been consistently raising their dividend for a number of years will continue to do so in the future. Think of the consequences if the company lowers or discontinues its dividend after distributing one for many years. The stock would almost certainly take a

significant drop. Generally, companies do everything in their power to
keep a level or rising dividend streak going. They are well aware what
kind of signal a dividend cut would give to the market. Discontinuing a
long streak of level or rising dividends generally means big corporate
changes are happening or that the company is struggling financially.

After determining that the company has consistently paid out a dividend offering a reasonable size yield, the main question the screener
needs to answer is if the company has the cash resources and is in a strong
financial position to continue paying rising dividends into the future.
There are financial tools and ratios that can be used to help determine
this. Investors should note, however unlikely it seems, that companies
that have historically paid out dividends in the past and are in a strong
position to be able to do so in the future may decide not to, for their own
reasons. Dividend policy is ultimately a corporate decision.

The key to being able to pay out a distribution is having strong cash
flow. Earnings are nice, but cash pays dividends. Investors should try to
screen for companies that have a consistent or growing operating cash
flow per share. A company that is able to grow its cash flow is clearly in
a better position to pay out a dividend than one that does not consistently generate cash.

A helpful measure in determining if the dividend is safe is the
dividend coverage ratio, which is calculated by dividing the trailing
12 months' operating cash flow per share by the last or expected
12 months' dividend. If the ratio returns a value significantly greater
than 1.0, an investor should feel confident that the dividend is secure.
If the ratio has a value below 1.0, it means that the dividend is clearly
at risk of being cut going forward. A company with a dividend coverage ratio below 1.0 needs to borrow or sell off assets to pay the dividend. Many companies in this position reduce or forgo the dividend
payment. If a screener does not have access to cash flow numbers, a
margin of safety for a dividend can also be achieved when the dividend
is less than two-thirds of earnings. Some independent financial firms
such as Standard & Poor's, Moody's, Value Line, and VectorVest offer
dividend safety ratings.

In addition to looking for a firm that has the resources to pay the dividend, an investor should be looking for firms that can possibly increase
their distributions. The *dividend payout ratio* shows the percentage of a
firm's earnings that are allocated to paying dividends. Any company

with a dividend payout ratio of less than the approximate market average of 0.41 may be a candidate for increasing its payout and, in turn,
shareholder returns. Also, if the firm keeps this ratio steady over time
and increases its earnings, the dollar amount of dividends received by
investors will rise.

Simply put, corporations with stronger earnings have an opportunity
to offer higher dividends than firms with weaker earnings. It's also more
likely that dividend-paying companies with strong earnings can, over
time, offer capital appreciation. This, when combined with dividend
income, can lead to an impressive total return.

When screening for winning dividend stocks it is important to determine that the company has a solid balance sheet. The economy goes
through boom and bust cycles. A dividend investor wants to feel comfortable that no matter what the business conditions are, the selected
stock will be able to pay out its distribution. These types of investors
should favor companies with low debt levels and readily available cash.
If need be, you want the company to be able to borrow to support its operations and its dividend. A company with high debt loads may find it difficult to borrow from its bankers, which in turn may threaten dividend
payouts.

Dividend stocks should also have access to short-term cash and
lines of credit. A company that has a significant cash position and is
able to maintain its current ratio above 1.0 should be able to satisfy this
requirement.

Standard & Poor's provides some quantitative measures that can be
helpful to investors focused on dividends. Along with Moody's and Fitch,
Standard & Poor's provides credit ratings on most firms that issue debt.
Credit analysis focuses on a company's ability to repay its obligations. It's
an easy step to take to say that a company that has a strong debt rating is
in a better position to pay its dividend than one with a lower rating.

Another helpful metric from Standard & Poor's that can be used as
a filter to help evaluate dividend-paying stocks is the Earnings and
Dividend (Quality) Ranking. This measure evaluates common stocks
based on historical long-term earnings and dividend performance. The
rankings are generated by a computerized ranking system based on per-
share earnings and dividend records of the most recent 10 years. This
period is long enough to measure significant secular growth, capture
indications of basic change in trends as they develop, encompass the full

peak-to-peak range of the business cycle, and include a bull and bear market.

Basic scores are computed for earnings and dividends and then adjusted as indicated by a set of predetermined modifiers for change in the rate of growth, stability within a long-term trend, and cyclicality. Adjusted scores for earnings and dividends are then combined to yield a final ranking.

Standard & Poor's has provided rankings on earnings and dividends since 1956. Portfolios of stocks with high quality rankings outperformed the S&P 500 and also outperformed portfolios of stocks with low Quality Rankings over the 1986–2002 period. A+ is the highest ranking a company can receive, while C indicates a relatively weak performance. The portfolio with the highest quality (A+) equities outperformed the S&P 500 by almost 1.5 percent annually. Investors should be aware that Quality Rankings are not intended to predict stock price movements.

A dividend-focused investor should not ignore the capital appreciation portion of a stock's total return. Although dividend stocks are less volatile than nonpayers, their values still move up and down each trading day. There is no guarantee that the stock will hold or increase its value during the period one owns it. Even if the stock is yielding a healthy dividend and is in a strong position to increase it going forward, if the stock price declines, the investor will not be pleased.

Dividend investors should screen for stocks that appear to be attractively valued and have the potential to move up in price. Investors who have the time and knowledge should do their own stock analysis. If not, they should look at filters of how brokerage and independent research firms rate the stock.

Lastly, two simple quantitative measures can be helpful in determining if a dividend stock is worthy of purchasing. Investors should look at the company's recent stock performance. Recent sharp price declines that offer seemingly high current yields should be avoided by dividend seeking investors. Often, companies with sharp declines lower or eliminate their dividends going forward. An investor should also look at the historic volatility of a stock through its standard deviation. A dividend-focused investor wants the standard deviation of the stock to be low. The stock should not have wild day-to-day price gyrations.

EXAMPLES OF HIGH DIVIDEND SCREENS

Below, you'll find some examples of screens for dividend stocks. Like the screens in the other chapters, unless specified, all the screens have stocks traded on U.S. markets, are priced no less than five dollars, and have a market capitalization of at least $100 million.

Stocks with High and Consistently Rising Dividends

The screen in Figure 7-4 filters for stocks that have a yield of at least 3.5 percent, which is approximately double the yield of the S&P 500. Each of the stocks has raised their dividend for 10 straight years. Finally, all the stocks are ranked at least four stars by Standard & Poor's equity analysts. Over the next 6- to 12- month period, four-star stocks are expected by S&P to be above average performers, and five-star stocks are expected to be the best performers. With a high yield, strong independent equity ranking, and a long history of raising dividends, all the stocks returned by this screen are certainly worthy of further inspection by dividend-seeking investors.

Strong Yield Combined with Strong Financials

The screen in Figure 7-5 filters for stocks with high yields plus strong financials. To qualify, a company needs to have a yield of 4.5 percent or more, which represents greater than double the dividend yield offered by the S&P 500. In addition, to show that it is in good financial shape it needs to have an attractive current ratio and debt-to-equity valuation. The current ratio needs to be at least 2.5, which means a company's current assets are more than twice its current liabilities. The debt-to-equity ratio needs to be in the lowest quartile; no higher than 4 percent. And finally, the stock needs to have a price of at least five dollars and a market capitalization of at least $1 billion. Investors looking for stocks that pay dividends will find these stocks to be good candidates to research further.

Dividends That Were and Continue to Be Safe

The screen in Figure 7-6 filters for stocks that yield 2.5 percent or more. The dividend appears safe going forward, which is reflected in its dividend coverage ratio of 2.5 percent (the market median) or more. Finally,

FIGURE 7-4 Stocks with high and rising dividends.

*Search Criteria	Low Value	High Value
U.S. Markets		
Price of Stock	$5	
Market Cap	$1 billion	
Dividend Yield	3.50%	
Dividend % Up last 10 years	100	
S&P Stars Ranking	4	

Output

Symbol	Company	Price of Stock	Market Cap in Millions	Dividend Yield	Dividend % Up last 10 years	Stars Ranking
MO	Altria Group	63.96	125,413	4.78	100	4
ASO	AmSouth Bancorp.	25.08	9,197	3.86	100	4
CBL	CBL & Associates Prop.	71.22	2,384	4.26	100	5
FR	First Industrial Rlty Tr.	38.88	1,740	6.83	100	4
HR	Healthcare Realty Tr.	36.86	1,941	6.34	100	4
HPT	Hospitality Properties Trust	44.49	3,091	6.26	100	4
HU	Hudson United Bancorp.	37.20	1,770	3.56	100	4
MAC	Macerich Co.	59.35	3,722	4.14	100	4
NCC	Natl City Corp.	36.37	24,611	3.73	100	4

*Screen was run on AdvisorInsight.com.

FIGURE 7-5   Stocks with high yield and strong financials.

*Search Criteria	Low Value	High Value
U.S. Markets		
Price of Stock	$5	
Market Cap	$1 billion	
Dividend Yield	4.50%	
Debt/Equity	0	4
Current Ratio	2.5	

Output

Symbol	Company	Price of Stock	Market Cap in Millions	Dividend Yield	Debt/Equity	Current Ratio
ACAS	AM Cap Strategs	33.00	2,826	8.85	0.71	3.44
ARA	Aracruz Cel-ADR	33.30	3,439	6.09	0.71	2.51
BPT	BP Prudhoe Bay	49.50	1,059	12.48	0.00	4.17
CUZ	Cousin Prop Inc.	30.50	1,519	4.85	0.44	7.44
HCN	Health Cr Reit	34.86	1,827	6.88	0.22	21.83
SFI	Istar Finl Inc.	43.35	4,828	6.44	1.88	30.07
IMY	Grupo IMSA-ADR	26.10	1,634	4.96	0.22	3.60
LXP	Lexington ppty	21.47	1,041	6.52	1.12	10.79
NFI	Novastar Finl	48.15	1,297	11.63	3.76	11.65
PFP	Premier Farnell	6.49	1,177	5.02	1.98	2.79
SAXN	Saxon Cap Inc.	23.18	1,155	7.42	0.00	9.03
TRO	Telecntro O ADR	9.26	1,170	5.54	0.07	2.77

*Screen was run on Zacks Screener.

FIGURE 7-6   Stocks with safe dividends.

*Search Criteria	Low Value	High Value
U.S. Markets		
Price of Stock	$5	
Market Cap	$100 million	
Dividend Yield	2.50%	
Dividend Coverage	2.5	
S&P Quality Rank	A–	

Output

Symbol	Company	Price of Stock	Market Cap in Millions	Dividend Yield	Dividend Coverage	S&P Quality Rank
CMTY	Community Banks, Inc.	26.98	344	2.52	2.5	A
EQT	Equitable Resources, Inc.	57.83	3,727	2.63	3.0	A–
THFF	First Financial Corporation	31.60	473	2.53	2.8	A
GMT	GATX Corporation	26.93	1,461	2.97	2.8	A–
JP	Jefferson-Pilot Corporation	50.65	7,094	3.00	2.5	A+
NCC	National City Corporation	36.09	24,611	3.88	2.7	A
STI	SunTrust Banks, Inc.	70.37	27,393	2.84	2.6	A+
PHC	The Peoples Holding Company	31.91	288	2.63	2.5	A
TRMK	Trustmark Corporation	27.21	1,797	2.94	2.5	A

*Screen was run on Fidelity.com

the companies have been historically enjoying consistent dividend and earnings growth, which is reflected in a S&P Earnings and Dividend Ranking of at least an A–. These quality stocks appear likely to continue to pay out an above average dividend going forward, which would make dividend-seeking investors very pleased.

Dividend Stocks in Poor Financial Health

The screen in Figure 7-7 shows companies that investors focusing on dividends should avoid. They have market capitalizations of $1 billion or more, dividend yields of at least 3 percent, and poor Standard & Poor's bond ratings of BBB+ or less. Each of the firms has struggled over the past five years. In that time period, they have only raised their dividend percentage and earnings per share a maximum of two of the last five years. A few of the stocks returned by the screen do not have a credit rating. Investors looking for dividends may want to look at other stocks to place their investment dollars.

High Dividend Stocks for the Wrong Reasons

Investors should be cautious of the dividend-paying stocks in Figure 7-8. For the last 26 weeks these stocks have significantly underperformed the market, have returns at least 10 percent less than the return on the S&P 500 in that period, and the consensus brokerage opinion on them is a hold rating or lower. This underperformance seems part of the reason that these stocks have high dividend yields of 4 percent or more. Going forward, one has to question whether the dividend is safe. Investors seeking equities that pay high dividends should probably pass on stocks returned by this screen.

POINTS TO REMEMBER

▶ Many investors are attracted to dividend stocks because of the income they provide and their perceived stability.

▶ Dividend payers tend to outperform in bear markets and underperform in bull markets.

▶ Companies that have been paying dividends for a number of years are likely to continue paying them in the future.

FIGURE 7-7   Dividend stocks to avoid.

*Search Criteria	Low Value	High Value
U.S. Markets		
Price of Stock	$5	
Market Cap	1 billion	
Dividend Yield	3.00%	
Credit Rating		BBB+
Earnings per Share Up Last five years		40%
Dividend % Up Last five years		40%

Output

Symbol	Company	Price of Stock	Market Cap in Millions	Dividend Yield
ALE	Allete Inc.	40.94	1,086	3.27
T	AT&T	18.51	15,169	4.98
CRE	Carr America Realty	32.24	1,797	6.06
CEI	Crescent Real Estate Eq	17.46	1,781	8.21
DPH	Delphi Corp	7.94	5,062	3.10
MYG	Maytag Corp	16.73	1,672	3.41
NHP	Nationwide Health Prop	22.40	1,582	6.23
NXL	New Plan Excel Realty Tr	26.05	2,779	6.09
NWL	Newell Rubbermaid	23.00	6,647	3.47
SWX	Southwest Gas	24.54	916	3.23
TAC	TransAlta Corp	15.40	2,916	5.51
WR	Westar Energy	22.38	1,964	4.02
WXH	Winston Hotels	11.57	312	5.08

Symbol	Company	Credit Rating	EPS % up last 5 years	Dividend % up last 5 years
ALE	Allete Inc.	BBB+	40	40
T	AT&T	BB+	40	20
CRE	Carr America Realty	BBB	40	40
CEI	Crescent Real Estate Eq	BB−	40	20
DPH	Delphi Corp	BB+	20	40
MYG	Maytag Corp	BBB	40	20
NHP	Nationwide Health Prop	BBB−	20	40
NXL	New Plan Excel Realty Tr		40	40
NWL	Newell Rubbermaid	BBB+	40	40
SWX	Southwest Gas	BBB−	20	20
TAC	TransAlta Corp	BBB−	40	40
WR	Westar Energy	BB+	20	20
WXH	Winston Hotels		20	20

*Screen was run on Advisorinsight.com.

FIGURE 7-8 High dividend stocks that underperform.

*Search Criteria	Low Value	High Value
U.S. Markets		
Price of Stock	$5	
Market Cap	$1 billion	
Dividend Yield	4.00%	
26-Week relative performance	Low as possible	
†Analyst Buy/Sell rating	3	

Output

Symbol	Company	Price of Stock	Market Cap in Millions	Dividend Yield	26-Week Relative Performance	Analyst Buy/Sell rating
T.BCE	BCE Inc.	29.68	27,340	4.0	110.7	3.0
EOP	Equity Office Pptys Tr	28.67	11,513	7.0	109.6	3.3
MMC	Marsh & McLennan Cos Inc.	31.52	16,730	4.0	71.5	3.2
MRK	Merck & Co. Inc.	30.69	68,789	4.7	67.7	3.0
PGN	Progress Energy Inc.	43.72	10,907	5.2	106.3	3.1
RD	Royal Dutch Pete Co NY	55.69	112,220	5.3	109.1	3.3
SBC	SBC Communications Inc.	24.72	82,189	5.0	105.1	3.0
SBC	SBC Communications Inc.	24.73	82,189	5.0	105.1	3.0
TLS	Telstra Ltd Spon ADR Final	18.40	46,624	5.4	105.5	3.0
WM	Washington Mutual Inc.	41.85	36,320	4.0	106.9	3.1

*Screen was run on Businessweek.com.
†1=Strong Buy, 2=Moderate Buy, 3=Hold, 4=Moderate Sell, 5=Strong Sell.

97

▶ A high dividend yield does not automatically mean a high dividend payout.

▶ The key to being able to pay out and increase dividends is stable and growing cash flow.

▶ A dividend-focused investor should not ignore a stock's capital appreciation potential.

SCREENING FOR MOMENTUM

Financial genius is a rising stock market.

—John Kenneth Galbraith

A LAW OF PHYSICS says that a body in motion tends to stay in motion. Momentum investors are firm followers of this principle. They look to buy equities with strong stock price momentum and are generally not particularly interested in the fundamentals and business strategy of a company. They do not even care if the company is profitable or what industry it's in. They focus solely on the price movements and chart patterns of a company's stock.

Momentum investors look for where the action is in the stock market and try to take advantage of it. An investor with a momentum philosophy is essentially riding a wave of recent good news with hopes that positive performance will continue. Followers of this strategy believe that one reason this method works is because of the reluctance of investors to sell winners. During the Internet and technology bubble in the late 90s, momentum investing worked tremendously, only to come crashing down in 2000, 2001, and 2002.

Given their predilection for going with the flow, as it were, momentum investors are not long-term investors looking to hold on to a stock for five years, riding out the inevitable ups and downs of the business cycle. They are short-term traders looking to make a fast buck, buying and holding a stock for a short time period and selling it to make a quick profit. They rarely hold on to a stock longer than a year.

If an investor is right about a momentum stock, it will provide the fastest move in the shortest time of any of the investment styles. Unfortunately, if one is wrong, the drop in stock price can be equally fast. An investor following this strategy has to be plugged in and very attuned to what's happening in the market on a day-to-day basis. One moment's price action may prompt an investment decision that has to be made.

Of course, momentum investors are aware that stocks are subject to supply and demand issues. Regardless of anything else, if the demand for a stock is outpacing the supply of available shares, the price will go up. Likewise, if the supply of the stock is greater than the demand, the price will decline. In the short term, the quality and valuation of the stock is not important in determining the price point where supply and demand meet.

FACTORS TO CONSIDER WHEN SCREENING FOR MOMENTUM STOCKS

Investors focusing on momentum look for stocks that have been the recent best performers, avoiding like the plague stocks that are making new lows. They follow the saying, "The trend is your friend," buying stocks that are going up and selling stocks that are moving downward. It is a very simple approach to understand. In fact, in the book *What Works on Wall Street*, author James O'Shaughnessey found that if you bought the top 10 percent of large capitalization stocks based on recent stock performance over the past 12 months, you would have consistently beat the S&P 500 over the next year. Furthermore, he discovered that if you bought the bottom 10 percent of large caps with the biggest price drops over the last 12 months, you would have underperformed the market over the following year.

Momentum players sometimes look at the measure of a stock's absolute performance over a time period. The problem with this method is it doesn't reveal how a stock has done compared to the rest of the stock universe. The *relative strength* measure solves this problem. It is the main measure that a price momentum player should look at.

Relative strength compares a stock's performance to the overall stock universe over a specific time period. A stock with a 200-week relative strength of 50 means that over that time period it outperformed half of all stocks. Relative strength for momentum is best used for recent time periods. A time frame of no less than a week and no more than 13 weeks should be used. A screener should focus on stocks that have a relative strength of 80 or above. The screener should set a target at what relative strength point they would sell the stock. Generally, when the relative strength has fallen 10 percent from the original screened-for relative strength point, it's a good idea to think about liquidating the position.

To strengthen the decision to buy a stock based on momentum, investors should also look at some stock data items and technical indicators. The recent chart pattern should show a clear up trend. Flat and up and down patterns do not cut it for momentum investors. The stock should be above its month and 13-week moving averages. When stocks fall below their moving average, it's a signal that the momentum has stopped.

Martin Zweig, a well-known investor and author, has said, "Big money is made in the stock market by being on the right side of major moves. I don't believe in swimming against the tide." Some screeners offer a technical ranking if individuals are not comfortable with looking at charts. Investors should read the screener's glossary to see how this technical ranking is derived.

Volume for the stock should be high and increasing during the recent up movement. High volume combined with a stock jump is sometimes interpreted to mean there was some conviction to the recent move. Furthermore, stocks with recent insider and institutional buying may indicate that there will be investors who may want to jump on the bandwagon and buy its shares.

Momentum investors need to have a quick trigger finger, selling out of a stock when the recent buying stops. As fast as investors pile into momentum stocks, they get out even quicker. They sell without hesitation and ask questions later. A momentum investor doesn't want to be caught holding a stock while all the other momentum players are selling.

Investors have to be the most vigilant with small and micro cap issues with not a lot of shares outstanding. Investors stuck holding these stocks while the momentum players are heading to the exits will experience gigantic paper losses. Momentum investors have to know at what point they're going to sell a stock. They need to decide for themselves at what percentage up or down they will sell. These percentages should be determined before the stock is ever purchased. This helps reduce the emotional element in the decision to sell.

If an investor is using a momentum strategy, it would be wise to look at earnings momentum, along with price momentum. William O' Neil, the publisher of *Investors Business Daily*, is a big proponent of combining earnings growth and momentum. Momentum investing will never be confused with fundamental investing—where an individual investor or portfolio manager looks at the underlying business and valuation to determine whether a stock is a worthwhile investment. Earnings momentum occurs when companies have had earnings percentage gains in recent quarters. Investors who combine price and earnings momentum generally look to buy stocks in the eightieth percentile and above, and sell when they break below the eightieth percentile.

Investors Business Daily publishes information about earnings and price momentum on individual stocks on a daily basis. Putting in an earnings component improves the quality of issues that are returned by a screen, compared to one with only a price momentum filter. Rising earnings may be the catalyst that is causing investors to buy the stock in recent time periods.

WEAKNESSES OF MOMENTUM

The momentum strategy has many aspects that an investor should be concerned about. For one, it's an investing style that tends to have high turnover. A strategy with a lot of trading means that brokerage commissions are going to pile up. Also, investors are likely to pay short-term capital gains on most of the stocks that are sold at a profit instead of long-term capital gains, which are taxed at lower rates. These factors will cut into the overall return an investor receives on an investment.

The other main fault with momentum investing is that it is not based on the valuation or any type of fundamentals for the corporation. It does not look at how the company's financials stack up against its competitors.

Very low quality and expensively priced stocks can be selected by a momentum screen. As long as an equity is rising, there is a possibility it may be picked up by momentum screeners.

There is also a higher probability of fraudulent activity involved with the trading of momentum stocks, especially with small and micro cap issues. These stocks are more subject to pump and dump scams, situations in which they are hyped up by con men who then turn around and sell their own shares at their zenith. Individual investors in these cases are usually left holding shares that are worth significantly less than when they purchased them.

Momentum investing is held in low regard by academics. The majority of them believe the stock market is fairly priced. According to many finance professors, the price of a stock is supposed to reflect all the relevant information available at that specific point in time. They argue that all securities are efficiently priced. And, in contrast to this viewpoint, momentum investing is based on the theory that trends exist and can be exploited. Academics believe that this simplistic style is performance chasing and that those who engage in it will not outperform the market in the long run.

Regardless of one's opinion of momentum investing, there is no denying that a portion of the investing public use it in some degree. Using price momentum as the only criteria is probably not wise. Combining price momentum with earnings momentum can give an investor some interesting stocks to do a further analysis on. Overall, momentum is best used as a factor within a growth, value, or GARP screen, and including relative strength could be a useful filter to finding winning stocks. In the eyes of many, selecting stocks that have some wind at their backs is preferable to selecting ones that have the wind blowing in their face.

FACTORS TO CONSIDER WHEN SCREENING FOR MOMENTUM

Like the screens in the other chapters, unless stated, each one of the following screens will have filters so that stocks will all be priced at five dollars or above, have market capitalizations of at least $100 million, and trade on U.S. exchanges. After selecting stocks based on momentum screens, an investor should run them more often than other stock selections because the names that are returned will probably change more often than those based on most other investment strategies.

Positive Momentum That Looks Good Near-Term

The stocks on the screen in Figure 8-1 have positive price momentum. They each have a 13-week relative strength of 80 or higher, meaning that in the past 13 weeks they have outperformed 80 percent of the stock universe. Each stock has a favorable technical reading measured by a proprietary S&P model. The stocks also have had recent insider buying, which may provide an impetus for some investors to follow suit and purchase the company's shares. Lastly, all the stocks are ranked at least four stars (accumulate) by Standard & Poor's analysts, showing that besides looking good technically, the companies returned by the screen are

FIGURE 8-1   Positive momentum that looks good near term.

*Search Criteria	Low Value	High Value
U.S. Markets		
Price of Stock	$5	
Market Cap	$100 million	
S&P Stars Ranking	4	
13-Week Relative Strength	80	
†Technical Rating	3	
‡Insider Activity	3	

Output

Symbol	Company	Price of Stock	Market Cap in Millions	S&P Stars Ranking
CHH	Choice Hotels Intl	58.85	1,916	4
ERTS	Electronic Arts	59.30	18,833	4
GIS	General Mills	52.35	18,937	4
HUM	Humana Inc.	32.42	4,733	5
SPF	Standard Pacific	64.50	2,144	5
WLP	Wellpoint Inc.	120.04	34,546	5

Symbol	13-Week Relative Strength	Technical Rating	Insider Buying
CHH	85	3	3
ERTS	86	3	3
GIS	80	3	3
HUM	96	3	3
SPF	88	3	3
WLP	93	3	3

*Screen was run on Advisorinsight.com.
†Technical Rating: 1=Unfavorable, 2=Neutral, 3=Favorable.
‡Insider Activity: 1=Unfavorable, 2=Neutral, 3=Favorable.

viewed as attractive by an independent research firm on a fundamental basis as well.

Price and Earnings Momentum

The screen in Figure 8-2 filters for equities that have price and earnings momentum. The price momentum is shown by each of the stocks having a 13-week relative strength of 80 or more. Each of the companies have raised their earnings per share (EPS) percentage for each of the past five years. Each stock returned by the screen has had low volatility over the past year, which is measured by a Standard & Poor's proprietary model. Finally, there is a filter that the average brokerage ranking (of 5) for the stock is a strong buy. The stocks returned by this screen are worthy of further inspection by investors interested in the momentum style.

Strong Recent Absolute Performance

The screen in Figure 8-3 filters for equities with a market cap of at least $1 billion that have performed well recently. The stocks need to have a minimum of a 10 percent return in the last four weeks and a 20 percent return in the last 12 weeks. Wall Street still believes these stocks can rise, with the minimum current average broker recommendation a moderate buy. At least five analysts from brokerage firms are covering these stocks and providing buy or sell recommendations. The stocks returned by this screen would certainly qualify as momentum stocks.

POINTS TO REMEMBER

▶ Momentum investors focus on the price movement and chart pattern of a stock.

▶ Momentum investors play off supply and demand issues for a stock.

▶ The relative strength of a stock is an important measure for momentum players.

▶ Investors should look at earnings momentum as well as price momentum.

▶ Momentum investors need to stay abreast with the market on a day-to-day basis.

FIGURE 8-2 Price and earnings momentum.

*Search Criteria	Low Value	High Value
U.S. Markets		
Price of Stock	$5	
Market Cap	$100 million	
†Average Broker Ranking	5	
13-Week Relative Strength	80	
EPS% Up Last 5 Years	100	100

Output

Symbol	Company	Price of Stock	Market Cap in Millions	Average Broker Ranking	13-Week Relative Strength	EPS % Up Last 5 Years
CYH	Community Health Sys	29.47	2,432	5	80	100
COO	Cooper Cos	75.23	2,310	5	80	100
HORC	Horizon Health Corp	29.45	155	5	93	100
HOV	Hovnanian Enterpr Cl'A'	50.27	3,054	5	94	100
ORCC	Online Resources Corp	8.64	137	5	94	100

*Screen was run on Advisorinsight.com.
†Average Broker Ranking of 5 is highest in Advisor Insights rating scale.

FIGURE 8-3   Strong recent absolute performance.

*Search Criteria	Low Value	High Value
U.S. Markets		
Price of Stock	$5	
Market Cap	$1 billion	
Average Broker Ranking		2
Number in Rating	5	100
% Price Change(4 Weeks)	10	
% Price Change(12 Weeks)	20	

Output

Symbol	Company	Price of Stock	Market Cap in Millions	Average Broker Ranking
ATVI	Activision Inc.	21.43	2,982	1.91
CHS	Chicos FAS Inc.	51.67	4,614	1.95
ETP	Energy Transfer	60.26	2,685	1.83
JOE	St. Joe Co.	69.06	5,249	2.00
PENN	Penn Natl Gaming	67.25	2,737	2.00
PPC	Pilgrims Prid-B	34.45	2,293	2.00
SHPGY	Shire Pharm Grp	35.57	5,732	1.17
TOL	Toll Brothers	73.64	5,574	1.93
WWCA	Western Wire-A	37.57	2,721	1.91

Symbol	Number In Rating	4 Weeks % Price Change	12 Weeks % Price Change
ATVI	22	10.35	52.53
CHS	20	12.82	32.52
ETP	6	11.20	20.76
JOE	7	13.88	37.02
PENN	12	12.33	59.47
PPC	6	12.11	28.98
SHPGY	6	14.30	24.11
TOL	14	10.89	59.29
WWCA	11	29.73	27.36

*Screen was run on Zacks.com.

▶ The main fault with the momentum method is that it has no valuation component.

▶ Overall, momentum is best used as a component in a growth, value, or GARP screen.

9

SCREENING FOR STOCKS IN SPECIFIC SECTORS

Investors operate with limited funds and limited intelligence, they don't need to know everything. As long as they understand something better than others, they have an edge.

—*George Soros*

ESIDES ALLOWING investors to search for potential stocks using bottom-up analysis, screening allows investors to look for potential investments using top-down analysis.

Some investors are interested in mining for companies that are in specific sectors. For example, they may be looking to buy a pharmaceutical stock or a bank stock. Buying equities in different sectors offers some diversification benefits. Often, people have a strong knowledge in a certain line of business because of their work responsibilities or a special interest and they try to transfer this expertise into successful stock picking. In many cases these same people do not know how to adequately evaluate a company's overall financial position and compare it to its competitors. They may also have difficulty realizing that a good company does not always translate into a good stock. The famed investor Warren Buffett once stated:

> Intelligent investing is not complex, though that is far from saying that it is easy. What an investor needs is the ability to correctly evaluate selected businesses. Note that word "selected." You don't have to be an expert on every company, or even many. You only have to be able to evaluate companies within your circle of competence. The size of that circle is not very important; knowing its boundaries, however, is vital. (See http://www.berkshirehathaway.com/letters/1996.html).

FACTORS TO CONSIDER WHEN SCREENING SECTORS

The first step to take when investing in specific sectors is determining the actual sectors the companies are in. In some cases this is not self-evident and requires a little research. For example, Federal Express and United Parcel Service are classified in the Industrial sector, REITs are classified in the Financial sector, and eBay Inc. and Amazon.com are classified in the Consumer Discretionary sector by some data providers.

Standard & Poor's, in collaboration with Morgan Stanley Capital International, developed a classification system called the Global Industry Classification Standard. GICS is composed of 10 sectors, 23 industry groups, 59 industries, and 122 subindustries. A company is assigned to a single GICS subindustry based on the definition of its primary business activity as determined by Standard & Poor's and MSCI. Revenues, earnings analysis, and market perception are a significant factor in defining principal business activity.

GICS was developed in response to the financial community's need for one complete, consistent set of global sector and industry definitions. The classification of a company in GICS is not set in stone. Over time, the classification for the specific company can change and/or new classifications can emerge. Dow Jones and Zacks also offer classification categories for companies.

For stocks in certain sectors, different ratios and financial measures should be stressed. Each sector has some unique factors that affect it. A few of the differences between sectors are:

- Different cost structures

- Different types of customers
- Different needs and uses of technology
- Different number and intensity of competitors

Screening allows the investor to compare firms in the same or similar businesses. Combined with an investor's own knowledge of an industry, screening can be an extremely helpful tool in finding attractive stocks to further research.

There are some sector specific ratios and statistics that are not available on commercial screeners. Some examples are the book-to-bill ratio for semiconductor stocks and research and development costs for drug companies. Investors may have to use outside sources to get specific data on sectors, and this information may be difficult and time consuming to obtain. Although the amount of specific industry measures that screeners have are limited, generally there is enough information on a screener to weed out the best stocks in a sector and point the investor in the right direction in his or her search.

EXAMPLES OF SECTOR SCREENS

Individuals can do screens based on any industries or subindustries, which can be seen in the screens we'll look at below. We note what screening criteria can be used to help investors choose equities that are well positioned for the future. When screening for stocks with certain characteristics in a specific sector, the number of equities returned will generally be smaller than other types of screens because the overall universe of stocks to draw from is smaller.

Banking Stocks

As seen in Figure 9-1, the Financial sector currently represents the largest percentage of any sector in the S&P 500. It accounts for close to 21 percent of the S&P 500.

The Banking subindustry in the Financial sector is a popular place where people invest. When interest rates are low or expected to decline in the near future, stocks in the banking sector are generally expected to perform well. The spread between the rate they lend out and borrow money widens in a low interest rate environment, which offers the

FIGURE 9-1   GICS Sector weightings.

	12/31/04 S&P 500
Consumer Discretionary	11.9%
Consumer Staples	10.5%
Energy	7.2%
Financials	20.6%
Health Care	12.7%
Industrials	11.8%
Information Technology	16.1%
Materials	3.1%
Telecommunication Services	3.3%
Utilities	2.9%
	100.00%

opportunity for higher profits. Banks today hedge some of their interest rate exposure, but for the most part when interest rates go up, these stocks underperform.

Most of these stocks return some of their earnings back to their shareholders in the form of dividends. Banking stocks generally have an above average dividend yield, especially the large money center banks such as Citibank, JP Morgan Chase, and Bank of America.

When screening for banking stocks, certain measures and ratios found on most screeners can be helpful in finding attractive stocks going forward. A banking stock should have a strong balance sheet, and this can be exemplified by having a good credit rating. It is best that borrowing costs be as low as possible. A banking stock should have a debt rating above A+. Banks with lower borrowing costs clearly have an advantage in this sector.

The return on assets and return on equity ratios for a stock in this sector should have a positive trend. The return on equity and return on asset ratios are a good way to evaluate management's performance. In the three months ended March 31, 2004, the industry average ROA was 1.38 percent, according to the Federal Deposit Insurance Corp (FDIC). Banks with higher asset sizes tend to have higher ROA ratios. In the first quarter of 2004, average ROA was 1.02 percent for banks with assets of less than $100 million; 1.19 percent for banks with assets between $100 million and

$1 billion; 1.33 percent for banks with between $1 and $10 billion in assets; and 1.45 percent for banks with more than $10 billion in assets.

Return on equity, also a profitability measure, is normally much higher than ROA. Typically, ROE ranges from 10 to 25 percent. In the first three months of 2004 the industry's average ROE was 14.86 percent. Financial institutions that rely mainly on deposits and borrowing to support assets, rather than on shareholders' equity, tend to have higher ROEs than those that do not. An unusually high ROE versus ROA can indicate that the bank's equity base is too small compared with its debt; this high leverage may limit its borrowing ability and growth prospects in the future.

In the opinion of most analysts, the price/book ratio is the single best valuation measure to evaluate a bank stock. Assets are easy to evaluate for banking stocks, making the book value more helpful as a valuation tool than in most other industries. A banking stock with a lower price/book ratio is generally more attractively valued. Banking stocks are affected by forces outside their control, such as interest rate changes. Over the long term, the best banking stocks will be those that have attractive valuations and are in strong financial shape.

The screen in Figure 9-2 looks for stocks that are in the GICS industry group: banks. They need to have a market cap of $1 billion or more and priced at least at five dollars a share. All appear attractively priced, with strong profitability trends. Each of the stocks has a five-year average price/book ratio below 10, so they appear to be a good value. In addition, their return on equity percentage has been up at least four of the last five years, and the return on assets is above 1.38, which is approximately the average for banks. Banks with these characteristics are worth further investigation by investors interested in buying a stock in this sector. Only two stocks were able to pass these filters.

Real Estate Investment Trusts

Another distinct subindustry in the financial sector that some investors like to invest in is Real Estate Investment Trusts (REITs). Over the past few years, these trusts have outperformed the market; the average REIT has risen 74 percent since late 1999.

Investors like the exposure that these securities give to the real estate market without having to own property directly. One doesn't have to worry about mortgage payments, mowing the lawn, and pipes bursting

FIGURE 9-2   GICS Industry group: Banks.

*Search Criteria	Low Value	High Value
U.S. Markets		
Price of Stock	$5	
Market Cap	$1 billion	
GICS Industry Group = Banks		
ROA (5-Yr Average)	1.38	
P/B (5-Yr Average)		
ROE (% Up Years Last 5)	80	10

Output

Symbol Company	Price of Stock	Market Cap in Millions	ROA (5-Yr-Avg)	P/B (5-Yr-Avg)	ROE (% Up Last 5 Years)
VLY Valley Natl Bancorp	26.62	2,730	1.55	3.83	100
WABC Westamerica Bancorporation	55.19	1,857	2.08	5.28	100

*Screen was run on Advisorinsight.com.

114

with REITs. REITs are much more liquid than actual physical real estate since they are traded on stock exchanges every business day of the year. They also have the attraction of a low correlation to the rest of the stock market, providing some diversification to an equity portfolio. Most REITs are currently classified as value stocks.

Currently, there are approximately 200 publicly traded REITs with a combined total market capitalization of approximately $180 billion. There are REITs that focus on a specific geographic region and on certain property types. For example, some REITs just have shopping outlets, and others have properties that are exclusively located in the Washington, D.C., area.

Most REITs are classified as equity REITs, which are companies that own and sometimes operate income-producing properties such as hotels, apartments, and shopping centers. Mortgage REITs are engaged in the business of financing real estate. Hybrid REITs are a combination of equity and mortgage REITs, owning property and making real estate loans.

In his book, *A Random Walk Down Wall Street,* expert investor Burton Malkiel states that he likes REITs because they allow investors to own assets (apartments, shopping centers, and office buildings) that cannot be duplicated elsewhere in the financial markets. Malkiel recommends keeping at least 10 percent of one's portfolio in REIT shares, and considerably more as one gets older and needs income.

Unlike corporations, REITs do not have to pay income taxes if they meet certain Internal Revenue Code requirements. To receive the benefit, a REIT must distribute at least 90 percent of its taxable income to its shareholders and receive at least 75 percent of that income from mortgages, rents, and sales of property. The result is that REITs tend to have high dividend yields; the average yield for a REIT is currently about 5.5 percent.

Besides the absolute dividend, investors should look for equities that are consistently raising their dividends. They should also look for stocks that have high payout ratios from *funds from operations,* which is a better measure than earnings for REITs because it excludes depreciation. The rationale for this is that real estate tends to appreciate over time, as opposed to other types of assets, making conventional earnings numbers misleading.

Investors looking for REIT stocks should search for companies with low debt levels and high credit ratings. The interest coverage ratios should indicate whether there is enough cushion to easily make debt payments. Companies with these characteristics will have much more financial flexibility going forward. Companies with high S&P quality rankings (earnings and dividend rankings) in this sector are desirable because most REIT investors want their stocks to have a history of meeting earnings projections and paying dividends consistently.

Try to find REITs with a diverse group of properties, because that reduces the risk of a problem with a specific property. Screening filters cannot determine the effect of a recession in a specific geographical area or a downturn in a certain sector of the economy. A REIT that has various properties would be in a better position to withstand sector specific problems or geographic slowdowns, which unfortunately inevitably happen.

The screen in Figure 9-3 filters for stocks in the GICS Industry group called Real Estate. The minimum market cap is $1 billion, which eliminates small and micro cap stocks. Dividends, as noted above, play a big role for investors who decide to invest in REITs. All of these stocks were screened for a yield of 5 percent or more and increasing their dividends paid per share in each of the last five years. And they all have a Standard & Poor's quality rank of B+ or better, which shows that they each have a strong history of earnings growth and paying out dividends.

Utility Stocks

The Utility sector is another area for investors who seek equities with high yields. Their dividend yields are usually between 3 and 7 percent. Utilities generally have low growth rates and very large capital expenditures to support their plant and equipment costs. When looking for utility stocks, an investor should look for companies with large and consistent dividend payments, a business that is stable, and one in a good geographical and favorable regulatory area.

When screening for a utility stock, an investor should try to ascertain if the company will be able to support and/or improve its dividend. One of the main reasons people invest in utility stocks is because of the dividend. The average electric utility has a dividend yield of about 5 percent. If the dividend is likely to be cut, a utility stock will generally have a sharp price decline. As stated earlier, the key to being able to pay

FIGURE 9-3 GICS Industry group: Real Estate.

*Search Criteria	Low Value	High Value
U.S. Markets		
Price of Stock	$5	
Market Cap	$1 billion	
GICS Industry Group = Real Estate		
Earnings & Dividend Rank	B+	
Yield %	5	
Dividends % Up Last 5 Years	100	100

Output

Symbol	Company	Price of Stock	Market Cap in Millions	Earnings and Dividends Rank	Yield %	Up Last 5 Years Dividends %
CLP	Colonial Properties Trust	37.55	1,076	Above Average (A–)	6.82	100
DRE	Duke Realty	32.74	4,868	High (A)	5.45	100
FR	First Industrial Rlty Trust	38.65	1,740	Above Average (A–)	6.83	100
HR	Healthcare Realty Trust	37.02	1,941	Above Average (A–)	6.34	100
HME	Home Properties	41.27	1,441	Above Average (A–)	5.86	100
LRY	Liberty Property Trust	40.41	3,699	Above Average (A–)	5.65	100
CLI	Mack-Cali Realty	43.72	2,801	Average (B+)	5.47	100
WRE	Washington REIT SBI	31.00	1,415	Above Average (A–)	5.04	100

*Screen was run on Advisorinsight.com.

out a distribution is having cash flow. Investors looking to put money in utility stocks should try to screen for companies that have a consistent or growing operating cash flow per share.

A favorable debt rating is desirable for a utility stock. It is an indication that the balance sheet is strong and that the company is in good financial health. The company should be profitable, which can be measured by the return-on-equity ratio. For most utility firms, return on equity ranges between 10 and 13 percent. A return on equity sharply below 10 percent may mean that there are some concerns with the company's underlying business. An ROE well above 13, on the other hand, may mean an increase in regulatory scrutiny may be coming, especially if its regional competitors' ROEs are much lower.

Two valuation measures that can be helpful in evaluating utilities are the price/book and price/earnings ratios. Most utility stocks normally trade between one and two times the company's book value per share. The forward P/E ratio for these stocks tends to be between 9 and 15. Utilities are generally priced at a discount compared to other sectors because of their slow growth nature. Utility stocks with price/book and price/earnings ratios far below other utility stocks may be an indication that the company has some facilities that are not economically viable anymore and/or some other serious business problems.

The screen in Figure 9-4 mines for companies in the Utilities industry classification. Each one needs to have a dividend yield of 4 percent or more to be included. These stocks are profitable and attractively valued, with a return on equity of at least 8 and a price/book ratio between 1.0 and 2.0. Finally, they were screened for having a debt-to-equity ratio as low as possible. Generally, because of their capital intensive nature, utilities tend to have a lot of debt, so this filter tries to select utilities that have lower debt loads compared to their peers.

Pharmaceutical Stocks

At one time or another, many investors have sought to find winning stocks in the Pharmaceutical sector. Many view pharmaceutical stocks as defensive. Demographic trends of an older population, the overall need for health care, and scientific advances attract many investors to these stocks. It is clear that there are outside influences in this sector that are impossible to screen for, such as patent approvals, government regulations and threatened price controls, and lawsuits. Even so, there is enough

FIGURE 9-4   Utilities sector.

*Search Criteria	Low Value	High Value
U.S. Markets		
Price of Stock	$5	
Market Cap	$500 million	
GICS Sector = Utilities		
% Debt/equity	Low as possible	
Dividend Yield	4	
Price/Book	1	2
ROE	8	

Output

Symbol	Company	Price of Stock	Market Cap in Millions	% Debt Equity
AEE	Ameren Corp.	49.45	9,698	106.8
CIN	Cinergy Corp	40.20	7,344	139.3
DTE	DTE Energy Co	43.26	7,567	157.3
EDP	EDP Energias De Portugal S A Spons ADR	29.27	10,490	135.8
KSE	Keyspan Corp	38.89	6,263	131.5
NI	Nisource	22.79	6,036	144.7
PGN	Progress Energy Inc.	43.62	10,860	139.2
SPI	Scottish Pwr Plc ADR Spons Final	31.40	14,504	110.4
UU	United Utils PLC ADR Sponsored	24.64	6,864	142.0
XEL	Xcel Energy Inc.	18.09	7,218	127.7

Symbol	Company	Dividend Yield	Price/Book	ROE
AEE	Ameren Corp.	5.0	1.7	9.7
CIN	Cinergy Corp	4.6	1.9	9.6
DTE	DTE Energy Co	4.7	1.4	10.3
EDP	EDP Energias De Portugal S A Spons ADR	12.1	1.2	8.3
KSE	Keyspan Corp	4.5	1.7	11.5
NI	Nisource	4.0	1.3	9.3
PGN	Progress Energy Inc.	5.2	1.4	9.2
SPI	Scottish Pwr Plc ADR Spons Final	5.0	1.6	14.7
UU	United Utils PLC ADR Sponsored	6.7	1.5	11.3
XEL	Xcel Energy Inc.	4.2	1.4	10.3

*Screen was run on BusinessWeek Online Advance Scanner.

information on screeners to be able to find pharmaceutical stocks with the most potential.

In screening for stocks in this sector, it is preferable to look for those that have at least a $5 billion market cap. Size is a big advantage in this industry. It allows a firm to have the potential to provide more resources for research and development, handle all the drug trials and paperwork of an FDA approval, and have a sizable and well-coordinated marketing operation. Small drug companies are dependent on the success of one or two drugs. In this business, there are numerous variables that could impact a single drug's sales, many of which are out of a company's control. It is safer to own a stock that has a mixture of various drugs on the market and drugs in various stages of development. Even large pharmaceutical firms such as Merck can have a significant share decline due to problems with one large-selling drug.

Investors should try to find stocks in this sector that have a consistent high level of sales and high operating margins, good management, and resources for research and development. Companies with these trends will always create investment interest. Average operating margins in this industry exceed 30 percent, which is more than twice the level of the average company in the S&P 500. Investors should be aware that sometimes companies reduce their research and development spending to prop up their margins. Over the long run, this would not be beneficial to shareholders.

The best overall ratio to use for evaluating pharmaceutical stocks is the PEG ratio. Companies that have a high expected growth rate and are priced at reasonable levels should perform well over the long term. What makes this ratio particularly useful is that the expected growth rate component of the PEG ratio will be influenced by analyst's expectations of factors such as the company's drug pipeline and the effect of patent expirations. Obviously, analysts' predictions concerning growth rates are not perfect, but they can give a pretty good idea of the company's prospects for the immediate future. Pharmaceutical firms with lower PEGs than their peers should be closely looked at by investors who are considering putting money in this sector.

The stocks selected in this screen in the Drug sector (Figure 9-5) appear well-positioned for the future. Each has a minimum of a $5 billion market capitalization because size is important in this sector. Each of the stocks has a growth rate above the average for the industry and at least one and half times the overall market. The stocks appear attractive going forward, with a projected price/earnings ratio no greater than 30 and a return on equity of at least 10.

FIGURE 9-5   Drug sector.

*Search Criteria	Low Value	High Value
U.S. Markets		
Price of Stock	$5	
Market Cap	$5 billion	
GICS Industry = Drugs		
Forward P/E Ratio		30
Return on Equity	10	
Company/Ind Growth Ratio	1	
Company/S&P Growth Ratio	1.5	

Output

Symbol	Company	Price of Stock	Market Cap in Millions	Forward P/E Ratio
ABC	Amerisourcebergen Corp	57.48	6,523	12.80
AMGN	Amgen Inc.	63.12	79,460	22.00
AZN	Astrazeneca Plc Sponsored ADR	35.15	59,340	14.70
CAH	Cardinal Health Inc.	54.45	23,548	13.40
GENZ	Genzyme Corp Com-Gen Div	59.86	13,548	27.90
GILD	Gilead Sciences Inc.	33.25	14,481	28.80
PFE	Pfizer Inc.	24.60	188,124	11.50
SNY	Sanofi-Aventis Sponsored ADR	37.56	54,451	12.80
SRA	Serona S A ADR Sponsored	15.46	9,214	16.90
SHPGY	Shire Pharmaceuticals Group Sponsored ADR	35.85	5,737	15.00

Symbol	Company	ROE	Company/Ind Growth Ratio	Company/S&P Growth Ratio
ABC	Amerisourcebergen Corp	11.00	1.1	2.7
AMGN	Amgen Inc.	11.30	8.0	2.0
AZN	Astrazeneca Plc Sponsored ADR	25.70	1.3	2.7
CAH	Cardinal Health Inc.	17.80	1.0	2.5
GENZ	Genzyme Corp Com-Gen Div	10.80	4.0	1.5
GILD	Gilead Sciences Inc.	50.90	5.0	1.8
PFE	Pfizer Inc.	13.40	1.2	2.5
SNY	Sanofi-Aventis Sponsored ADR	36.30	1.5	3.0
SRA	Serona S A ADR Sponsored	18.50	5.0	1.7
SHPGY	Shire Pharmaceuticals Group Sponsored ADR	16.90	1.5	2.9

*Screen was run on businessweek.com.

Oil Stocks

Energy stocks have recently received a lot of attention by investors. Oil and natural gas prices have been at their highest level in a generation, with oil passing the $60 a barrel mark. Besides being the basis for heating homes and fueling vehicles, it is a raw material for products such as plastics, medicines, and paints. Even if oil prices should fall in the near future, it seems likely it will be some time before oil is at historically inexpensive levels.

Supply and demand issues seem to support high oil prices. The continuous huge demand in the United States plus the recent surge in demand in developing economies such as China and India should keep a solid support level for prices. In addition, most of the oil producing countries are not politically stable, which creates uncertainty and helps keep the price high. Many people focus on the oil producers in the Middle East in terms of geopolitical risk, but oil-rich countries outside that area are also concerns, such as Russia, Nigeria, and Venezuela. And finally, the turbulence in Iraq plus the threat of global terrorism adds an extra unofficial premium to the cost of oil. Terrorists and insurgents have tried and would love to disrupt the flow of oil to the West. They have in many cases burned oil wells and attacked energy convoys and pipelines.

Like pharmaceutical firms, large oil companies have a big long-term advantage. Oil is a homogeneous product; it is basically the same product for everyone. Consumers do not see much difference between the products offered by alternative sellers. There is no real distinction between ExxonMobil's oil and ChevronTexaco's. This makes it difficult for a company to gain brand loyalty. Large firms in this industry receive economies of scale in marketing, production, and exploration. They tend to have integrated operations, whereby they have less reliance on other energy firms. This provides them with a big cost advantage compared to smaller firms.

Like most commodity-based industries, traditional valuation measures are not very useful for oil firms. For example, price/earnings, price/book, and price/sales are not that meaningful for these firms. The actual price of oil is the overriding factor in terms of the valuation of these stocks. When oil prices are high, the explorers and producers are traditionally the best performers in the sector; when oil prices soften, the large integrated companies are usually the best performers in the group.

Overall, though, when oil prices are at high levels or are expected to rise sharply, the whole group benefits.

Profit margins are an important measure for oil stock investors to look at. Companies with higher margins in the industry are much better positioned to weather the ups and downs of the oil market. Margins in this sector are much firmer than sales.

The screen in Figure 9-6 searches for attractive stocks in the Oil Energy sector, according to Zacks. Each of the equities has annual sales of $1 billion or more and has a positive net margin. Each of the companies can meet immediate cash needs, which is shown by a current ratio of at least 1.0. Finally, they have been filtered for a "strong buy" or "buy" by at least 50 percent of the analysts who make recommendations, and a minimum of five analysts must provide buy, sell, or hold ratings. Investors looking for oil stocks may find some stocks returned by this screen worthy candidates.

Consumer Staples

Some investors are attracted to consumer staple stocks in these uncertain economic times. Consumers buy their products despite what is going on in the overall economy. Prices for consumer staples tend to be inelastic; the amount demanded by consumers is not much affected by price. People will purchase soap, beer, toothpaste, and cosmetics in good times and bad. Many investors feel comfortable putting money in these stocks because they have some familiarity with them. Generally, companies in this sector sell products that have recognizable brand names. While the average person may have a hard time explaining the intricacies of what a technology firm does to make money, it is not much of a mystery what Anheuser Busch's (BUD) business is.

In this sector, investors should seek companies with consistent sales growth and profit margins. Organic growth is preferable to growth that is the result of mergers and acquisitions. If the trend for revenues and margins are on the rise, it is an even better sign. Investors should look for valuation levels that are reasonable. Price-to-earnings and price-to-book levels that are very low generally indicate serious operational problems with the company. On the other hand, valuation levels that are very high are likely to be tenuous. Rapid growth and large widening of margins is rare in this sector. In most consumer staples' lines of

FIGURE 9-6   Oil-Energy sector.

*Search Criteria	Low Value	High Value
U.S. Markets		
Price of Stock	$5	
Market Cap	$1 billion	
Sector-Oils-Energy		
Number in Rating	5	
% Rating Strong Buy or Buy	50	
Net Margin	0.2	
Annual Sales	$1 billion	
Current Ratio	1	

Output

Symbol	Company	Price of Stock	Market Cap in Millions	Number in Rating	% Rating Strong Buy or Buy
APA	Apache Corp	51.63	16,856	27	55.6
BR	Burlington Resources	43.12	16,881	27	55.6
PPP	Pogo Producing	46.97	3,026	11	54.6

Symbol	Net Margin	Annual Sales in Millions	Current Ratio
APA	0.3	4,190	1.39
BR	0.3	4,311	2.24
PPP	0.3	1,162	1.79

*Screen was run on Zacks.com.

business, competition is fierce, which keeps companies in check. Coca-Cola versus Pepsi, and Procter & Gamble versus Colgate Palmolive, are a few examples of heated rivals in this sector.

The screen in Figure 9-7 searches for equities in the Consumer Staples sector. The stocks selected combine growth and value characteristics. Each has a five-year historical EPS growth rate of at least 16 percent, which is the average growth rate in the Zacks database for this sector. The companies selected have a price/book value of 2.5 or less and a price/cash flow level no higher than 12. If an investor is looking to buy a consumer staple stock, the ones returned by this screen appear to be worth some further analysis.

Retailers

Another industry group that consumers have a lot of familiarity with is retailers. We go into stores daily and buy items we need for everyday life. There's a big difference between retailers aimed at wealthy consumers and discount retailers. There is also a big difference between the financial characteristics of fashion and nonfashion retailers. Measures such as return on equity, profit margins, and inventory turnover can vary widely.

Retailers are clearly subject to general economic conditions that cannot be screened for. Employment levels, inflation rates, and the level of interest rates affect shopping trends. Investors should be careful evaluating overall sales numbers for retailers. A popular screening measure in investing is looking at annual percentage sales increases. The total sales number in retailing can be increased substantially just by opening new stores. A better measure is comparing same store sales numbers from one year ago. Good retailers squeeze more money out of existing stores. There are generally bad days ahead for any retailer whose same store sales are shrinking instead of growing.

Although they may sell different products that have different features, successful retail stocks generally have similar characteristics. It is important for companies in this industry group to have good relationships with their suppliers and customers. Investors should try to find retailers who have strong earnings per share growth that are priced at reasonable levels. A forward PEG ratio between zero and 1.0 would support these characteristics. They should look for firms that have low debt levels and satisfactory cash reserves. A proxy for the quality of the management can

FIGURE 9-7 Consumer Staples sector

Search Criteria

	Low Value	High Value
U.S. Markets		
Price of Stock	$5	
Market Cap	$1 billion	
Sector-Consumer Staples		
5-Year Historical Growth Rate	16	
Price/Book		2.5
Price/Cash Flow		12

Output

Symbol	Company	Price of Stock	Market Cap in Millions	5-Year Historical Growth Rate	Price/Book	Price/Cash Flow
ADM	Archers Daniels	22.66	15,270	23.10	1.96	10.49
BG	Bunge Ltd	55.97	6,223	33.27	2.37	10.47
BLC	Belo Corp. A	23.67	2,729	16.76	1.74	11.93
CCE	Coca-Cola Entr	21.45	9,741	42.92	2.16	5.54
FDP	Fresh Del Monte	29.15	1,690	48.08	1.77	6.11
PAS	Pepsiamericas	20.94	2,920	18.67	2.03	9.89

*Screen was run on Zacks.com.

be measured by looking at the return-on-equity ratio; high ROEs are preferable.

In this industry, management of inventory is very important. Companies selling lower end and inexpensive products should have high inventory turnover numbers. Inventory turnover is generally calculated by taking the cost of sales and dividing it by the average inventory. In evaluating the ratio, the emphasis should be on the company's performance compared to its peers. A very low inventory turnover ratio compared to its competitors usually means that capital is tied up in excess inventory and that there may be some outdated inventory. A very high ratio number may indicate efficiency, but it could also mean there is inadequate inventory for the prevailing sales volume. This can lead to back orders, shortages, and possibly lost future sales. Overall, retailers with a solid brand, aggressive marketing, and a mix of brick-and-mortar stores and Web sites will likely do well in the long run.

The screen in Figure 9-8 is for equities in the GICS Industry group sector called Retailing. Each of the stocks needs to have a price of at least five dollars and a minimum market cap of $1 billion. Each of these retail stocks exhibit a strong trend: In each of the last five years, their earnings per share, sales, and net profit margins have risen. With this type of recent financial performance, these retail stocks merit the attention of those interested in investing in this sector.

Semiconductor Stocks

We live in a world where technology is increasingly changing our everyday lives. From the way we do our personal banking to the way we get driving directions to go from one place to another, technology is altering the way we conduct our lives. The growth and the speed in which semiconductors process and perform certain tasks is one of the main drivers of the technological age we live in. These items are the size of a fingernail and can carry out millions of instructions in a few seconds. Many semiconductor companies focus on a specific type of chip for a specific type of application. Investors have to be careful, though, because product life cycles are short in this industry. Today's technology can quickly become obsolete.

Semiconductor stocks generally are growth stocks. They tend to have higher price/earnings ratios, higher price/book ratios, and higher growth

FIGURE 9-8 Retail sector.

*Search Criteria

	Low Value	High Value
U.S. Markets		
Price of Stock	$5	
Market Cap	$1 billion	
GICS Industry Group = Retailing		
EPS % Up Last 5 Years	100	100
Sales % Up Last 5 Years	100	100
Net Profit Margin Up Last 5 Years	100	100

Output

Symbol	Company	Price of Stock	Market Cap in Millions	Last 5 Years EPS % Up	Last 5 Years Sales % Up	Last 5 Years Net Profit Margin Up
BBBY	Bed Bath & Beyond	40.15	12,150	100	100	100
CHS	Chico's FAS	50.96	4,551	100	100	100
LOW	Lowe's Cos	55.91	43,205	100	100	100
MIK	Michaels Stores	29.91	4,031	100	100	100
UAG	United Auto Group	28.25	1,312	100	100	100

*Screen was run on Advisorinsight.com.

rates than the overall market. Investors should look at the PEG ratio to make sure the stock is reasonably priced compared to its predicted growth. An investor should try to focus on semiconductor stocks that have low PEG ratios compared to their competitors.

Companies in this sector tend to have more debt than the average company. Investors should make sure though that the debt is not excessive and is in line with other semiconductor stocks. Profit margins tend also to be above average. As in all types of sector investing, the investor should compare the profit margins of the firm to its peers.

A ratio that is not available on commercial screeners and is useful in determining whether the semiconductor sector is attractive is the book-to-bill ratio. This ratio is compiled by the trade association Semiconductor Equipment and Materials International (SEMI). It is calculated by dividing the value of the three-month average of global orders by the three-month average of global sales for North American semiconductor equipment companies. When the ratio is above 1.0, new equipment orders exceed shipment levels, indicating that chip manufacturers are raising spending rates for new production equipment. The opposite is true when the book-to-bill ratio is below 1.0 (Standard & Poor's *Semiconductor Industry Report*, July 29, 2004).

The screen in Figure 9-9 looks for stocks in the semiconductor subindustry. Each stock has a price/sales ratio no higher than 20. Price/Sales is a good valuation method for chip stocks because some companies in the industry do not have earnings. The stocks also have a positive trend, with increases in sales and profit margin in at least four of the last five years. Not one of the companies was able to increase these measures the last five years in a row. The Semiconductor sector is cyclical, so it's difficult to have sales and margins rising year in and year out. The companies returned by this screen appear to be well-positioned for possible future outperformance.

POINTS TO REMEMBER

▶ Before investing in specific sectors, an investor needs to determine the specific sector classification of a stock.

▶ For stocks in different sectors, certain ratios and financial measures should be emphasized.

FIGURE 9-9 Semiconductor sector.

*Search Criteria

	Low Value	High Value
U.S. Markets		
Price of Stock	$5	
Market Cap	$100 million	
GICS Sub-Industry = Semiconductors		20
Price/Sales		100
Sales % Up Last 5 Years	80	100
Net Profit Margin Up Last 5 Years	80	

Output

Symbol	Company	Price of Stock	Market Cap in Millions	Price/Sales	Last 5 Years Sales % Up	Last 5 Years Net Profit Margin Up
DIOD	Diodes, Inc.	21.00	292	2.11	80	80
ICST	Integrated Circuit Sys	19.42	1,365	5.55	80	80
INTC	Intel Corp	22.42	141,762	3.93	80	80
LLTC	Linear Technology Corp	37.21	11,425	13.85	80	80
MXIM	Maxim Integrated Prod	38.31	12,460	9.53	80	80

*Screen was run on Advisorinsight.com.

130

► Combined with an investor's own knowledge of an industry, screening can be a helpful tool in identifying attractive stocks for further research.

► Some industry specific ratios and statistics are not available on screeners.

10

STOCKS WITH NEGATIVE CHARACTERISTICS

In this game, the market has to keep pitching, but you don't have to swing. You can stand there with the bat on your shoulder for six months until you get a fat pitch.

—Warren Buffett

TOMMY ARMOUR, A famous golf pro, once said about improving a golf score, "It is not solely the capacity to make great shots that makes champions, but the essential quality of making very few bad shots." (*Financial Analysts Journal*, September–October 2004, 15). This advice applies to investing as well. Brokers, investors, and the financial media are almost always focused on telling people what stocks they should buy. Everyone is searching and hoping to find the next Microsoft.

Watch any financial program and the host invariably asks their portfolio manager or analyst guests for stock recommendations; rarely do you hear the question: "What should an investor sell?" Few financial people go on the record saying you should sell XYZ stock. Not many are willing to stick their neck out and say they think the XYZ Company is going to go bankrupt and its stock is going to be worthless within the next year. Few are actively searching for the next Enron.

A worthwhile endeavor for stock enthusiasts is to look for stocks to *avoid* buying, and for extremely aggressive investors to look for stocks to sell "short." A short sale is the sale of stock one doesn't own, with the intent of buying it back later at a lower price. In essence, it is borrowing a stock from another investor through a broker, selling it in the market, and subsequently replacing it. A short seller profits when a stock declines in price.

Used in isolation, short-selling is a risky strategy. In a straight long purchase of a stock, the maximum amount an investor can lose is the amount invested plus any brokerage commissions. A short seller's loss potential is unlimited, because the potential upside for a stock is infinity.

10 NEGATIVE CHARACTERISTICS

There are over 10,000 stocks listed on U.S. exchanges. Knowing which stocks to avoid can be as important as deciding which stocks to purchase. There are certain signs that a stock may not be a worthwhile investment. We have gathered them into a list of 10 characteristics that can be quantitatively screened, which would be viewed as big negatives for a company. These factors can be found on commercial screeners by anyone who has a personal computer with access to the Internet.

Investors should be aware that practically every company will have at least one of these negative qualities. No stock is perfect. We recommend avoiding any stock that has at least three of the 10 discrete characteristics—they are not   ranked in a particular order. There are a lot of fish in the sea, so why buy a stock with so many negatives when there are plenty of other possible good ones to choose from? As Warren Buffett has said, "The ability to say no is a tremendous advantage for an investor."

Companies with High Debt Levels

These companies are clearly in a less enviable position than companies with low debt. For high debt companies, there is always the requirement of paying back their creditors, which influences their business decisions. Firms with high debt have less financial flexibility. They have less and have to pay more for access to the capital markets.

Investors can screen for debt by looking at the debt-to-capital ratio and the debt-to-equity ratio. High values for these debt-related ratios, especially compared to their peer companies, is a big negative. A company with a debt-to-equity ratio above 50 should have a good business reason to justify having that level of leverage. Investors should be careful because some companies list a portion of their long-term liabilities in balance sheet entries that do not get picked up as debt. A company's ability to pay back its debt can also be seen in the company's credit or debt rating. Be wary of any company whose bond ratings are below investment grade in what is called "junk status."

Companies with Low Cash Levels

Cash is the lifeblood of a business. Companies that have a low level of cash and/or are unable to turn some of their assets into cash quickly will not be in business very long. Like companies with low debt, companies with high cash levels have far greater financial flexibility. They have more options when it comes to expansion, research and development, mergers and acquisitions, share buybacks, paying dividends, and reducing debt.

Cash levels can be seen in screens by looking at the current ratio and the cash-to-total-assets ratio. Investors should be cautious about investing in companies that have current ratios below 1.0 and cash-to-total-asset ratios less than 2 percent.

Stocks with Liquidity Concerns

The ability to convert a stock position into cash fast and at a reasonable cost is demanded by market participants. Stocks that are priced below five dollars and/or that have a market capitalization below $100 million do not offer good liquidity. Unless otherwise indicated, all the screens included in this book exclude stocks with these two characteristics.

Some individuals may be attracted to these stocks because they can buy more shares than they can of any current blue chip stock, and because many stocks with liquidity concerns are among the best performing stocks on any given trading day. Yes, there are a few of these companies that will go up exponentially, but there's a much greater chance of the stock depreciating and going bankrupt when it is priced below five dollars. Generally, companies with low market caps have low total sales, low or negative earnings, and/or have serious business problems. Investors should not gamble and invest in companies priced this low and with such low market caps. "Caveat emptor" when a stock is priced very low—there usually is a good reason for it.

Stocks with poor liquidity usually trade with a big percentage spread between the bid and ask prices. Equities with a low average volume of shares traded and those that do not have a lot of shares outstanding also have problems with liquidity. Stocks with few shares available will have low volume for obvious reasons; others will have low volume because there is just a lack of interest in them. If very few people want to buy a stock, it will have low volume. Investors should be weary of putting money in any stock that has an average daily volume of less than 100,000 shares.

Companies That Recently Went Public

All things being equal, it is preferable to own stock in a company that has been public for at least three years. The regulatory requirements of being a public company are much more stringent than that of a private company. A newly public company will have a steep learning curve just keeping up with the SEC documents, which they have to disclose each quarter.

Recent initial public offerings are difficult to evaluate and compare to other firms since they have little or even no history of financial performance. Firms that recently went public are also more likely to have a less experienced management team. A few of these stocks will rocket up in price and make their stockholders happy. All in all, though, investors generally would be better off investing in well-established companies than firms where there is much more uncertainty.

Some screeners allow an investor to screen companies by their initial public offering date. If a screener does not have this function, they can exclude recent initial public offerings by using any filter that requires three years worth of data, such as historical earnings per share growth.

Companies That Are Losing Money

Investors should avoid companies that do not have earnings. Firms, not in a commodity-based industry, that have gone several consecutive quarters without earning money should especially be avoided. Companies that continually lose money will eventually be out of business. Investors can spot these companies by looking for a negative net income figure and with negative historical and forward price/earnings ratios. These stocks will also usually have low net profit margins and low or negative return-on-equity ratios. Stocks with no earnings and without a clear business plan of getting to profitability may appreciate in short time spans based on hype, but in the long run stock returns correlate with earnings. Over time, strong earnings generally equals good stock performance.

Companies with Low Sales Levels

Before investing in an equity, an investor should make sure that it has a minimum of $100 million in annual sales. Companies that cannot satisfy this criterion are too volatile and risky to invest in. Without a significant amount of sales, a company would need to frequently raise new cash to meet expenses. Corporations need revenue coming into their coffers to survive. The way companies allocate money when they receive it is different from company to company. Without it, though, any company is living on borrowed time.

Sales are a cleaner figure than earnings, since it is harder for accountants to manipulate. Sales is the top line number. It is not affected by depreciation, interest expense, write-downs, taxes, etc. Besides looking at absolute sales numbers, investors should avoid companies that have bad sales trends. Avoid companies that have been unable to consistently increase sales and are not projected to do so in the future, especially when they're not in a commodity-based industry. Over time, it's better to own companies that are growing based on sales growth than on earnings growth. There's a limit to how much belt tightening and cost cutting a company can do. Although a company cannot have unlimited sales, there is generally a very high bar to reach before resistance takes place.

Companies with Low Projected Growth Rates

Stocks over the long term are valued based on the discounted value of their future cash flows. Over time, the rate at which the cash flows grow is a major determinant of whether a stock will outperform or underperform the overall market. Certain industries have higher sales and earnings growth rate projections than others. For instance, technology and biotech companies tend to have much higher growth rates than utility and industrial stocks. An investor should evaluate a company's growth prospects compared to its competitors. It is also important to make sure the growth projections are coming from at least five analysts. Forecasting growth is difficult, so having more opinions is preferable. Companies with growth rates forecasted by two or less analysts should be avoided by investors.

Companies with a Low Level of Institutional or Management Ownership

Investors feel more secure putting money in a stock that has other knowledgeable people also investing in it. The company's management and large institutions are two groups of investors whose stock purchases and sales are widely followed by potential shareholders.

A company's management should have the best information on the day-to-day operations of its business. It is not a good sign if they're selling large blocks of the company's stock. Of course, there may be some selling for diversification reasons by management, whose stock is an outsized portion of their net worth. Also, there may be some selling to help pay large personal expenses, such as mortgages and children's college tuition. But even so, an investor has to ask the question: "If management thinks the stock has such amazing prospects, why would they sell it at all?" Even though in some cases it may be difficult, managers could adjust their personal financial situations so it was not imperative to sell their company stock.

Potential investors also like seeing that institutional investors have purchased or are considering purchasing stock in a company. Some examples of institutional investors include mutual funds, pension funds, and large endowments. Institutions have many more resources than the average investor, have more access to the companies they invest in, and are able to spend a lot more money on research from Wall Street firms. If a representative of the California State Employees Pension Fund calls the CEO of a company with questions about its business strategy, the representative is much more likely to get an answer than if an individual investor places the same phone call.

Stocks That Do Not Pay a Dividend

In strong bull markets, dividends are afterthoughts for most investors. In stagnant and bear markets, investors tend to focus more on them. Studies have shown that, over time, dividends provide a big chunk of the market's total return. As mentioned previously, there used to be tax laws that favored capital gains over dividends. In recent legislation, the taxes on dividends have been given equal treatment to those of capital gains. Companies that pay out dividends are usually in better financial conditions than those that do not. They have enough extra cash to set aside to pay out directly to investors.

Through their dividend policy, companies provide guidance to how management sees future prospects. A company that raises its dividend believes that future earnings will be able to support it. And in most cases, a company that lowers its dividend is having financial difficulty. A dividend cut is usually met in the marketplace with a sharp sell-off in the stock. Overall and all things being equal, investors should want their stocks to pay dividends, rather than relying totally on capital appreciation to reach their goals.

Stocks with Expensive Valuations

Great companies may not be great stocks to own. Often, the best companies have expensive valuations. There are many metrics an investor can look at to see how a stock is valued. But whatever measures are used, it's important to compare the valuation to other companies in its industry and the market as a whole. Comparing General Motors valuation ratios to Ford Motors, for example, is more relevant than comparing them to Cisco Systems.

The best overall valuation method is the forward PEG ratio. This ratio incorporates three of the most important components in evaluating a stock: its price, its projected earnings, and its expected growth rate. Companies with forward PEG ratios below 1.0 are looked at as being attractively valued. Investors should be careful investing in any equity with a forward PEG above 2.

The weaknesses of the PEG ratio can be alleviated by supplementing it with other valuation ratios. With the price/sales ratio, a potential investor can evaluate companies that do not have earnings. Pretty much every company has some sales, but not every one earns money. A stock with a price/sales ratio above 2 is looked at as being expensive.

For investors concerned with earnings quality, an investor can look at the price/cash flow ratio. Cash flow is less subject to accounting adjustments than earnings. A stock with a price/cash flow ratio above 20 is looked at as being very highly priced.

A helpful tool to evaluate commodity and banking stocks is the price/book ratio. This is a good valuation metric for firms with easily defined assets. Generally, a price/book ratio above 5 is viewed as expensive. With all the valuation measures that have forecasted earnings and growth rates as a component, a potential investor should be cautious if there are less than three analysts covering the stock.

OTHER NEGATIVE INFORMATION

Unfortunately, screening can only pick up certain factors that can be detrimental to a stock. Many qualitative factors are impossible to screen for. One can alleviate this concern somewhat by screening to see how the analyst community feels about the stock. Hopefully, fundamental analysts take into consideration outside influences in their evaluation of an equity. If an investor wants to do his or her own homework on the fundamentals, there are many signs that a stock should be avoided.

A lot of negative qualitative information can be found in recent news stories about a corporation. Investors should be wary about companies getting away from their prime business either by themselves or through combinations. An example of this would be if Coca-Cola decided it wanted to go into the automobile manufacturing business. When a company gets away from its core competency, there's a much greater chance of failure.

Legal concerns are another factor that can have an enormous effect on share prices, though potential legal liabilities are difficult to quantify. The names Eliot Spitzer and Alberto Gonzales attached to news of an investigation into a company or industry is usually met with sharp selling pressure. Recently, the stocks of insurance, money management, and for-profit education groups were slammed when allegations against them were reported and investigations were made public.

Unfortunately, the market generally does not wait for "guilt" or "innocence" or "liability" or "no liability" verdicts to move the stocks downward. A lot of investors also follow the maxim "Where there's smoke, there's fire." In many cases, investors believe that allegations against a company are only the tip of the iceberg of their activities and what might come down the road in terms of litigation. Investors, if they can, should try to avoid companies that may have some legal problems.

Individuals have different knowledge bases and interests. They should try to invest in companies they can understand. They may not need to know intimate details of the company's financial statements, but they should have a basic understanding of the company's business. It is virtually impossible for an investor to make an informed investment decision on whether to buy or sell a stock if they have no idea how the company earns money.

Also, as noted earlier, before investing in a stock, an investor should have a good feeling about it. If a company is returned in a screen, passing all the filters, but you personally still have an overall negative opinion of it, you should walk away and not buy the stock. Never purchase a stock that you don't have a good gut feeling about.

POINTS TO REMEMBER

▶ Investors should try to avoid stocks that have some of these characteristics:

1. Companies with high debt levels
2. Companies with low cash levels
3. tocks with liquidity concerns
4. Companies that recently went public
5. Companies that are losing money
6. Companies with low sales levels
7. Companies with low projected growth rates
8. Companies with a low level of institutional or management ownership

9. Stocks that don't pay a dividend

10. Stocks with expensive valuations

▶ Knowing what stocks to avoid can be as important as knowing what stocks to buy.

▶ No stock is perfect; every stock will have some kind of negative quality.

SCREENING FOR
MUTUAL FUNDS

If you pay the executives at Sarah Lee more, it doesn't make the cheesecake less good. But with mutual funds, it comes directly out of the batter.

—Don Phillips, President, Morningstar

MANY INDIVIDUAL investors and some institutions believe they do not have the time or expertise to search for individual stocks or bonds. Instead they turn to one of the most popular investment vehicles to try to resolve these concerns: the mutual fund.

A mutual fund is a type of investment product that gathers assets from investors and invests them in individual stocks, bonds, or money market instruments. Mutual funds, essentially, pool money, and with the proceeds buy a number of securities and then divide them into individual shares. More than 80 million people, or one out of every two households in America, have some portion of their money invested in mutual funds. For most U.S. workers, mutual funds serve as the cornerstones of their 401(k) plans, IRAs, or other similar retirement accounts.

Mutual funds are a highly regulated product. A price is set on them based on the closing price of the securities in the fund at the end of a trading day (4:00 P.M. Eastern Standard Time). Even though they are composed of several securities whose prices change during the day, an open-end mutual fund only has one stated price per day, and generally an investor is only allowed to buy or sell an open-ended mutual fund based on its price at the end of the trading day.

In order to sell its shares to the public, a mutual fund must first register its shares with the SEC by filing a federal registration statement pursuant to the Securities Act of 1933. They also must file with each state (except Florida) in which the fund's shares will be offered. Further, broker-dealers and their registered representatives who sell mutual funds to the investing public are subject to regulation under the Securities Exchange Act of 1934, while investment advisors to funds generally must register under the Investment Advisors Act of 1940. The Securities Exchange Act requires that broker-dealers maintain extensive records, segregate customer securities in adequate custodial accounts, and file detailed annual financial reports with the SEC. The Investment Advisors Act contains various antifraud provisions and requires fund advisors to meet record keeping, custodial, reporting, and other requirements.

Mutual funds are required by the Securities Exchange Act to provide a fund prospectus to all prospective investors and to existing shareholders annually. The prospectus is an official document that describes the fund's goals, strategies, risks, performance history, and expenses. It also describes how to purchase and redeem fund shares. Information and statistics inside prospectuses form the core of the database for mutual fund screeners.

Mutual funds must also send shareholder reports to investors every six months, showing the fund's performance and its financial statements. Once per quarter they have to report their 10 largest holdings. Investors should examine any material they receive from the fund company regarding the mutual funds they own to make sure that the fund company is doing its best to meet the goals set in the prospectus.

Whether the mutual fund is an open- or closed-end fund determines if the fund can issue new shares. Most mutual funds are open-ended. The more money clients invest in the fund, the more shares are issued. These funds can continually create shares, and are required to redeem them at the current net asset value (NAV) at any time upon a shareholder's request. The NAV equals the underlying value of the securities that the fund owns divided by the number of fund shares outstanding, or in other words, it is the dollar value of one share of a mutual fund.

There are far fewer closed-end funds. These funds have a set number of shares, and the fund can be priced each day at a premium or discount to its actual holdings. These funds are traded on a stock exchange, similar to the way most individual stocks are traded. The market price of closed-end fund shares is determined by the supply and demand in the market. Both sets of these funds are professionally managed and may be invested in stocks, bonds, or a combination of them.

Today there are more mutual funds than there are stocks listed on the New York Stock Exchange. Presently, there are more than 4,600 managed equity funds. The table in Figure 11-1 shows the number of different types of mutual funds in 1984 and 2003.

FIGURE 11-1   Mutual funds table.

	1984	2003
Equity Funds	459	**4,601**
Capital Appreciation	306	2933
World	29	863
Total Return	124	805
Hybrid Funds	**89**	**509**
Bond Funds	**270**	**2,043**
Corporate	30	290
High-Yield	36	198
World	1	106
Government	45	316
Strategic Income	47	355
State Municipal	37	527
National Municipal	74	251
Money Market Funds	**425**	**973**
Taxable	329	661
Tax-Exempt	96	312
Total	**1243**	**8,126**

Data for funds that invest in other mutual funds were excluded.

FIGURE 11-2   Net assets of mutual funds (in billions of dollars).

	Sep-04
Stock Funds	$3,916.0
Hybrid Funds	478.9
Taxable Bond Funds	937.0
Municipal Bond Funds	326.3
Taxable Money Market Funds	1,597.7
Tax- Money Market Funds	295.4
Total	**7,551.2**

Data provided by the Investment Company Institute

The figure illustrates how much the mutual fund business has grown in recent years. With the huge amount of choices available, it is important for investors to be able to sort out good mutual funds from bad ones and funds that are appropriate for them from those that are inappropriate. All in all, the mutual funds that investors should consider purchasing have characteristics and properties that can be screened for. Screens can be used to help identify those funds that best fit the investor's needs.

The first mutual fund was the Massachussetts Investment Trust offered by MFS Investment Management in 1924. Obviously, since that time the industry has grown exponentially. Currently, there is more than $7 trillion invested in mutual funds. Figure 11-2 shows approximately how much money is in various types of funds.

Today, there are mutual funds with all types of investment styles and with all sorts of securities. The majority of mutual funds can be divided into five broad types:

- Equity funds
- Fixed income funds
- Hybrid funds (combination of equity and fixed income, sometimes called "balanced funds")
- International funds
- Money market funds

In these styles, there are a wide range of funds and many derivations of them. For example, in the equity style, there are funds that just invest in a specific sector like Information Technology, and there are others that invest in only what the fund classifies as small cap value stocks. In the fixed income area, there are funds that invest only in municipal bonds from a specific state, and others that invest in highly rated corporate bonds. Bonds funds can be divided into tax-exempt and taxable funds.

In the international arena, there are funds that invest in specific countries and geographic regions. Others apply an investment style, such as growth or value, with securities from all over the world. With international funds it is important to find out if a fund hedges or doesn't hedge its currency. This is important because currency returns can have a bigger impact on an international portfolio than stock selection.

Like bonds, money market funds also can be divided into tax-exempt and taxable funds. Tax-exempt funds should normally only be purchased by individuals in a top tax bracket. Money market funds are attractive to investors looking for liquidity, a high stability of principal, low risk, and a small amount of income generation.

In all these styles, investors can choose between active management funds—where portfolio managers make frequent buy and sell decisions on securities—and passive funds, which try to mirror the performance of an index such as the S&P 500 or the Russell 2000. The theoretical case for indexing begins with the premise that markets are efficient and all possible news is reflected in a securities price. As a result, indexers believe the only way that an active manager can add value to portfolio returns is to use material, nonpublic ("insider") information.

When trading, index fund managers do not need to worry about what securities to buy or sell—it is determined by the actions of the index itself. It is clear to anyone who wants to know what securities are in an index fund. This forces passive investors, however, to own bad companies as well as good ones and to own ridiculously expensive stocks as well as cheap stocks, just because they are in the index being tracked. A belief of index investors is that competition makes it extremely difficult to beat the overall market's returns consistently. Characteristics of active and passive funds are shown in Figure 11-3.

Active funds have higher costs and higher tax liabilities than passive funds. They have to pay for portfolio managers, analysts, and research, including any quantitative models that help them select securities. Index funds need much less staff and for the most part can have quantitative analysts and computers do most of the work. Mutual funds with active management have much higher turnover of securities. The annual turnover in the S&P 500 averages about 4 percent, while the traditional

FIGURE 11-3   Index funds versus active funds.

	Index Funds	Active Funds
Expenses	Low	High
Tax Liabilities	Low	High
Turnover	Low	High
Chance of Outperformance or Underperformance	Low	High
Transparency	High	Low
Cash Drag	Low	High

active U.S. equity portfolio averages 100 percent annually (*Journal of Indexes*, August–September 2004, 11). Thus, index funds delay capital gain taxes because they hold on to individual stocks much longer, which means some money that would have been paid out in taxes can keep producing investment returns.

Many consider active funds the "sexier" product because they offer the chance for market-beating performance. However, over long periods of time index funds, in fact, have had better performance. Nearly 90 percent of all active funds that have 10-year records have underperformed the overall market. Numerous studies have shown that star mutual fund managers are just as likely to underperform than outperform the market several years into the future. And there are studies showing that index funds have a 350 basis point advantage over the average active mutual fund due to management expenses, brokerage costs, sales charges, and tax advantages (*Journal of Financial Planning*, September 2002). Vanguard has become one of the largest mutual fund companies in large part due to their offerings of a variety of index funds.

Warren Buffett, one of the world's most famous and successful investors, is a big proponent of index funds. He has noted that:

> Most investors, both institutional and individual, will find that the best way to own common stocks is through an index fund that charges minimal fees. Those following this path are sure to beat the net results (after fees and expenses) delivered by the great majority of investment professionals (http://www.berkshirehathaway.com/letters/1996.html).

The Investment Company Institute reports that households continue to shift from holding stocks and bonds directly to holding them through mutual funds. Over the past decade, investors have poured billions of dollars into mutual funds because of some of the clear benefits that this financial product provides and due to the large sales forces and big-budgeted marketing efforts to sell them. Mutual funds offer numerous features that are attractive to investors.

A main selling point is that mutual funds provide diversification at a relatively low cost. Many only require as little as $250 to open and have expense ratios (management and related fees) of less than 1 percent. They have lower risk and volatility than an individual stock. Their day-to-day percentage price gyrations are lower than individual equities. And mutual funds have within them several securities so that if one position in the portfolio declines sharply, there are numerous other securities that can offset the loss. Generally, mutual funds should not have more than 5 percent of their portfolio in any one single security. Mutual fund holders can benefit from diversification techniques usually available only to investors wealthy enough to buy significant positions in a wide variety of securities.

Mutual funds also provide overall diversification for an investor's portfolio by providing numerous investment styles and security types, which can lower the overall risk of an investor's assets. If an investor wants to invest in diverse assets from REITs to international stocks at a reasonable cost, there is an assortment of funds from which to choose.

And there is professional portfolio management, which is attractive to the many individuals who lack the time, desire, and background to become experts in specific investment areas and to trade in the market on a daily basis. The people who manage mutual funds do it for a living. Their workday mainly consists of searching for underpriced securities to buy and overpriced ones to sell, and trading on their beliefs and analysis. Generally, money managers have high levels of education and a number of years of relevant work experience. They usually have expertise within a single investment style or vehicle.

In most cases, portfolio managers or their financial companies have access to vast amounts of financial information and statistics, contacts at companies they are considering investing in, and key personnel at their own firm to help them select securities for their mutual funds. If a portfolio manager calls a high ranking official of a company asking to speak about their firm's prospects in the future, they are much more likely to get a helpful response than a small individual investor who would make the same inquiry. Further, money managers have real-time access to crucial market data and are able to execute trades on a large and cost efficient scale. And finally, the interests of portfolio managers are often generally tied to that of the fund holders because they are usually compensated based on how well their fund performs.

Another reason investors are drawn to mutual funds is convenience. It is as easy as a phone call or a click on a mouse to buy or sell shares. Mutual fund net asset values are easily found in the business section of the newspaper, the Internet, or by calling the fund company's toll free phone number.

Liquidity is not a concern for mutual fund holders. By law, as noted above, investors are able to redeem mutual fund shares on a daily basis. Individuals can arrange to have automatic monthly investments added to their mutual funds by authorizing electronic fund transfers from a checking account in any amount and on any date they choose. Dollar cost averaging, where an investor puts in a certain dollar amount in regular intervals, helps reduce the chance of heavily investing in the securities market when it is at its zenith. It reduces market risk by acquiring more shares at low prices and fewer shares at higher prices. And because it is an automatic process, dollar cost averaging takes some of the emotional element out of investing and allows an investor to avoid the difficult game of trying to time the market.

Many of the fund companies have phone and branch representatives that can help guide individuals to funds that may be appropriate for their needs. Another bonus is that the fund companies take care of the laborious task of record keeping. For an individual investor to keep track of all the dividend payments, proxy statements, and capital gains and losses of dozens of individual securities would be a full-time job. Investors in mutual funds do not have to worry about where to store their physical bonds or stock certificates, since mutual funds maintain accounts on their books and send periodic statements showing all of a client's transactions.

Mutual funds can be a helpful financial planning tool. For example, some funds are geared for individuals who know they're going to have a large financial need in the future for life events such as retirement or a child's college tuition. These funds, sometimes referred to as "lifestyle funds," generally have a higher weighting in equity funds in the early years, and as the need date approaches, they become more conservative and shift to higher weights in short-term bond and money market mutual funds.

SCREENING MUTUAL FUNDS

Screening for mutual funds follows similar procedures and provides many of the same benefits as those of screening for stocks. Screening clearly saves time and money for an investor. Most fund screeners are available for free or at a nominal cost.

Without screening, an investor would have to get prospectuses or other information from a large number of funds and mull through them for the statistics important to them. With screening, an investor can go through a database of a few thousand funds and in a manner of seconds receive a small list of those with characteristics he or she is looking for. Screening puts each mutual fund on equal footing and returns those with characteristics an investor is seeking. By going through the process of screening for mutual funds, an investor will surely be learning about them and should become a more informed investor.

There are numerous Web sites where investors can screen for mutual funds. Some of them are listed on Figure 11-4.

Mutual funds screeners have fewer variables than stock screeners. A sample screener is shown in Figure 11-5.

Most mutual fund screeners have similar features. A user is able to pick from various filters, input parameters for the variables, run the screen, and see the mutual funds returned as output.

FIGURE 11-4   Web sites with mutual fund screeners.

www.cbs.marketwatch.com
www.forbes.com
www.mfea.com
www.money.com
www.moneycentral.msn.com
www.morningstar.com
www.quicken.com
www.screen.yahoo.com
www.smartmoney.com
www.zacks.com

FIGURE 11-5   Variables in mutual fund screeners.

Universe

Investment Style
Fund Family

Ratings

Independent Research Firm's Rating	min	max
Return Rating	min	max
Risk Rating	min	max

Performance Returns

Year-to-Date Return	min	max
1-Year Return	min	max
3-Year Return	min	max
5-Year Return	min	max
10-Year Return	min	max

Holdings

Net Assets	min	max
Median Market Cap	min	max
Average Credit Ranking	min	max
Average Maturity	min	max

Costs

Expense Ratio	min	max
Load	yes	no
Turnover	min	max

Search Now

The filters in screeners can generally be divided into five categories, which can be seen in the above figure. The Universe category allows an investor to filter broad characteristics of funds. In the Investment Style area in this category, an investor can segment funds by the strategy used by the mutual fund, such as large cap growth or stocks in the Health Care sector.

Another filter in the Universe category is the Fund Family. Some fund companies have millions of dollars of assets with thousands of employees, while others are one-man shops. A lot of people get a degree of comfort by investing with a well-known money management firm. This category allows investors to search for funds in a specific mutual fund family like Fidelity, Vanguard, and T. Rowe Price.

Some investors like to put money in a few mutual fund families. This saves on their individual paperwork, and sometimes when they have a certain amount of assets with one firm, they receive cost breaks. Fund families allow investors to easily move money from one mutual fund within their firm to another. Investors should be aware that such a switch from one mutual fund to another is a taxable event for accounts that are not tax deferred. Obviously, a screener will be constrained by the amount of mutual fund families in the database. Also, when the fund family is used as a filter, the results of a screen will be much smaller than if the whole mutual fund universe is used.

Another category in these screeners is Ratings. Standard & Poor's and Morningstar have independent rankings for mutual funds. Standard & Poor's mutual fund star ranking offers a quick gauge of how a fund performed relative to its peers. Funds are ranked within Standard & Poor's style categories using the Sharpe ratio, a measure of risk-adjusted performance. Five-star rankings are given to the top 10 percent that also outperform their benchmark over three years. The next 20 percent receive a four-star ranking; followed by the next 40 percent, which receive three stars; 20 percent receive two stars; and 10 percent receive one star. Funds that receive three stars or more must also outperform the three-month Treasury bill over three years.

Morningstar also has a five-star ranking system for mutual funds. They measure an individual investment fund's performance and risk, then calculate risk-adjusted rankings for three-, five-, and 10-year periods. Its overall star ranking is a weighted average of these three time periods. They award a five-star ranking to the top 10 percent in each of the three investment classes. The funds in the next 22.5 percentile receive four stars, those in the middle 35 percent earn three stars, those in the next lower 22.5 percentile receive two stars, and the bottom 10 percent only get one star. Morningstar rankings are updated every month.

There are also other individual quantitative return and risk rankings provided by other firms and available on screeners. Most of the risk rankings are based on the standard deviation of the fund, the measure of how widely the return of a mutual fund varies over time (both on the upside and downside). Independent ratings and ranking systems like those discussed above can be helpful, but they are not necessarily predictive of future performance. Each company has a different method of rating a mutual fund, so an investor should do his or her best to understand the independent firm's methodology.

The Performance category shows historical investment returns of mutual funds for different time periods. Past performance returns are an area that investors have always, rightly or wrongly, used to judge mutual funds. The three- and five-year time periods are the most relevant for a potential investor. Time periods shorter than this do not provide a long enough history for assessment. If an investor screens for funds with returns greater than 10 years, most funds will be excluded because they have not been in existence that long.

The Cost category, as its name suggests, looks at some of the various charges investors may face if they invest in a mutual fund. Expense Ratio relates to the cost of running and managing the mutual fund. Loads are a commission that brokers and financial advisors charge for selling a fund to a customer. All things being equal, it is better for an investor to buy a mutual fund with a low expense ratio and without a load. Funds from many money management companies, including Fidelity, Vanguard, and T. Rowe Price, can be bought directly through them without the use of a broker.

The Turnover filter shows how often a fund trades. An annual turnover of 50 percent means that on average the fund manager replaced 50 percent of the portfolio during the year. Turnover above 100 percent per year is usually looked at as being excessive. Large turnover can eat into performance returns and cause a high tax liability for fund holders. According to Morningstar, funds with extremely high turnover—400 percent or more—can generate costs of 8 percent or higher to a fund's overall return.

Finally, the Holding category looks at characteristics of the specific securities in the portfolio. The Net Assets filter shows how large a mutual fund is. Small cap mutual fund investors often do not want to see their mutual funds grow to a large size; efficiency in buying small cap stocks becomes an issue for the fund. Also, it is more difficult for the large funds to find enough quality small cap stocks to purchase. Often, when small cap funds reach a large asset size, they close themselves from accepting new investment dollars. They may or may not open again at a later date.

The Median Market Cap acts as a proxy to see what the average market cap of the equities in the mutual fund are. This can show if the fund is true to its investment size and style. For example, it can serve as a check to see that a fund that states it is a large cap fund is in fact actually a large cap fund.

Screens that incorporate fixed income mutual funds generally have filters for the average maturity and credit ranking of the bonds in the portfolio. Fixed income investors are usually concerned about the safety and quality of the bonds in a mutual fund and when they are scheduled to mature.

STEPS TOWARD BUYING A MUTUAL FUND

Before searching for mutual funds to possibly buy, investors should ask themselves what they want out of the investment, assessing their tolerance for risk, their time frame, the return they would be satisfied with, and so on. Then there are the questions about particular funds, which screening can help elucidate: its type and characteristics. Of course, you should have a clear idea as to what you are looking for in a fund. But your involvement doesn't end there, or at least it shouldn't. The wise investor needs to keep an eye on his or her investments, which is where the screens can be of use again, along with other forms of information. Let's go into all of this.

What Are Your Investment Goals and Objectives?

Before putting money into any mutual fund, you should decide what you want to achieve. Funding a retirement, a child's college education, and money for large purchases such as a house and car are the goals of many investors. Don't put money into mutual funds without a plan and an idea of how much money is needed and how the money is going to be used. You'll need to determine the time frame for when you'll need the money and how much risk you're willing to take. Investors who need money in a short period of time will want to invest in very safe instruments. Those with a longer time frame can take on more risk.

Another goal of many investors is diversification. Depending upon the types and concentrations of your other investments, adding certain types of mutual funds can help you reduce the risk in your overall portfolio. For instance, gold funds, emerging market stock funds, and REIT funds tend to have a low correlation with the U.S. stock market, and they might be trending up, or at least remaining steady, when the market is trending down and negatively affecting the other funds in your portfolio. Also, mutual funds themselves provide diversification by holding many securities that are pooled together and sold as a single individual asset.

What Kind of Funds Best Meet Your Needs?

An investor who needs money from a mutual fund in a short period of time should invest in extremely low risk items such as money market or short-term bond funds. If this is your situation, safety of principal should be your primary concern since you'd need to have assets that are liquid and, of course, you don't want to lose any value.

If, on the other hand, you have a time frame of more than five years, you could consider putting some of your money into higher risk vehicles, such as domestic and international equity funds. The long period of time before it is needed offers a tremendous chance for the investment to grow. An occasional decline will most likely be offset by other gains. Capital growth and inflation protection are very important to investors with longer time frames.

Equity funds offer high return possibilities but also come with high volatility. A general rule of thumb of financial planning is: The longer an investor's time frame—the more risk he or she can afford to take.

Another factor that may affect your mutual fund choices is taxability. In most cases, the type of funds you have in a taxable account should be different from those in a tax-deferred account. For example, municipal bond mutual funds should never be in a tax-deferred account. Aggressive equity funds where the portfolio manager does a lot of trading and which subsequently have a high turnover are more appropriate for tax-deferred accounts.

Figure 11-6 illustrates long-term characteristics of various types of mutual funds.

FIGURE 11-6   Long-term characteristics of mutual funds.

Stock Funds	Capital Gains Potential	Income Potential	Total Return Potential	Risk Level
Aggressive Growth	Very High	Low	Very High	Very High
Growth	High	Low	High	High
Income	Low	High	Moderate	Moderate
Growth/Income	Moderate	Moderate	Moderate	Moderate
Industry Specific	Varies	Varies	Varies	Varies
Precious Metals	High	Low	Varies	High
Global	High	Moderate	High	High
International	Very High	Low	High	High
Fixed Income Funds				
High-Grade Corporate	Low	High	Moderate	Low
High-Yield Corporate	Very High	High	High	Very High
U.S. Government	Low	Moderate	Moderate	Low
Municipal Bond*	Low	Moderate	Low	Low
Money Market	Very Low	Low	Low	Very Low

*Income potential and attractiveness of municipal bonds partly depends on investor's tax situation.

Source: Standard & Poor's.

What Fund Characteristics Are Important?

After determining the type of mutual fund to invest in, investors have to weigh the characteristics that are most important to them in terms of shopping for a specific fund. For some, manager experience may be the most important variable. For others, it may be cost, which can be represented by the expense ratio and whether the fund has a load or not. It is an individual decision as to what factors are most important to an investor. Every investor is unique.

Put in the Parameters and Run the Screen

Before putting in values for the variables, an investor should check to see how they are defined by the screener. Different screeners may have different definitions for their variables. As opposed to looking at equities, there are much fewer variables to choose from in screening for mutual funds. It is sufficient in most cases to have parameters that are simply greater than or less than a certain number. The only variable where a range could be helpful is mutual fund size.

If you're screening for a mutual fund with less than $5 billion in assets, there's a chance that a screen will return mutual funds with a very low level of assets. It's preferable for a mutual fund to have at least a minimum of $100 million in assets before placing money in it. If after running a screen the output is too high, you should tighten the parameters or add another filter. If too few funds are returned, loosen the parameters or remove a filter. Ideally, a mutual fund screen should yield between three and 10 fund names that an investor can put through some further inspection and analysis. Generally to run a worthwhile mutual fund screen, you don't have to screen for more than four variables.

Select Mutual Funds to Purchase

This is the step where you make the decision to buy a specific mutual fund. You should look at the mutual funds returned by a screen as the starting point, but besides looking at the screening results from quantitative filters, you should consider some qualitative factors as well.

Certain investors may choose to stay clear of some fund families that have been tainted recently because of improper trading by their portfolio managers and/or favoritism shown toward some large fund holders. There are some investors who would rather invest with a large fund company because of the perceived comfort and service level provided, rather than a small portfolio management firm, regardless of the firm's performance records and costs.

Investors should also be aware when the mutual fund distributes capital gains, interest income, and dividends. This usually occurs toward the end of the calendar year, and fund holders are taxed whether they bought the fund a day before the distributions or bought it 10 years ago. Try to avoid buying a mutual fund just before the record date, to avoid unnecessary taxes, keeping more of your money in your pocket. Why pay taxes on an investment when you did not even receive the benefits from the capital gains?

Investors need to weigh what they consider the most important factors are for a mutual fund. Cost, adherence to investment style, and manager tenure are significant. And before investing, you should read the fund prospectus and double check to make sure that the screening variables that returned the fund as output are in fact accurate. That is, you should make sure that the fund is what it claims to be. Just because a mutual fund has "large cap" or "value" in its name doesn't mean that the portfolio manager is buying stocks with these characteristics.

You should also compare the mutual fund's rankings against its peer group. Morningstar, Lipper, Standard & Poor's, and others can be used for these comparisons. These companies have publications that are available in most public libraries. There's no harm in trying to learn as much about a mutual fund as possible before committing money to it. And of course you should have a comfort level with any investment you make.

Finally, buy the mutual fund directly from the company managing the fund. By avoiding using a broker or investment advisor to place the buy or sell transaction, you can save up to 5 percent of the total investment. Why pay a commission or load when you don't have to?

Follow Up Afterward

Screening is an early step in the investment process. Your involvement does not end after you've selected a fund. Save the prospectus and keep tabs on the fund's performance, comparing it to funds with similar investment styles. When the fund releases what the actual holdings in it are, you should check to see that they adhere to the fund's stated investment style. As you (hopefully) did before purchasing the fund, once again verify that the fund is what it claims to be. For example, if an investor invested in a health-care fund and the largest holding is now in Wal-Mart stock, it should raise a red flag.

You should also make sure that the same portfolio manager is still managing the fund. Like the screening process for individual stocks, run the mutual fund screen periodically (preferably quarterly) to see if the fund has the same characteristics that you initially screened for. And by running the screen from time to time, it may give you reason to think about possibly selling a fund or you may pick up some other fund names that you might be interested in buying. This helps instill discipline in the screening process.

Overall, investors should exercise some patience and be in mutual funds for the long term. They are not vehicles that should be bought and sold frequently. Unless there are significant changes in the investment style or philosophy of the fund or there's a manager change, you should hold the fund for at least three years. Three to five years is a reasonably fair period of time to judge a manager's performance. A recent study showed that mutual fund owners, in general, churn their accounts so much that they have reduced their returns by an average of 20 percent over the past decade. Peter Lynch has stated that many investors in his outstanding performing Fidelity Magellan Fund did not get the results they hoped for because they were buying and selling the fund often, and at the wrong times.

Besides looking at the fund's performance against a standard benchmark such as the S&P 500, to get a better look at how a fund is doing an investor should judge them against mutual funds of the same investment style. It is also best to judge the fund in good and bad markets.

THE COST FACTOR

When screening for mutual funds, there are certain characteristics that investors should emphasize. Cost is a primary factor to consider. Similarly to the way an investor in commercial real estate should focus on location, location, and location, an investor searching for mutual funds should look at cost, cost, and cost.

Costs are an important focus because they are more permanent in structure and not likely to change substantially in the short term. There's no way to know how a mutual fund will perform in the coming year, but you can get a pretty good idea of what the cost of investing in the fund will be.

Loads

In mutual funds, costs come in many forms. When investors purchase a fund through a broker or investment advisor, they pay a load. Different types of funds have different charges to cover the cost for advice you receive in selecting the fund. Each share class has different sales charges and different fee structures. The basic definitions of the shares classes are:

- *A shares* are sold with an initial (front-end) sales charge that is usually between 3 and 5 percent and is deducted from the initial investment. These funds usually also charge a 12b-1 marketing fee, which is usually around 23 basis points and is deducted from the fund's assets each year. The 12b-1 fees are named for the section of the Investment Company Act that permitted them.

- *B shares* do not have a front-end load, but carry a redemption fee or back-end load if the shares are redeemed within a certain number of years. The back-end load declines every year until it disappears (usually after six years). B shares carry 12b-1 marketing fees, which are typically higher than those on A shares.

- *C shares* are known as "level-load" shares. They do not have front-end or back-end sales charges. They have 12b-1 marketing fees, which are charged as long as you own the fund.

- There are other classes of funds, but they are generally variations of A, B, and C shares.

As a general rule, investors should not buy a fund with a load. The only scenario in which investors should even consider buying a load fund is if they have absolutely no investment knowledge and need the assistance of a broker or financial planner. In this case, the load can be seen as the cost of financial advice. The investor should be aware that the load will be a big hindrance to their overall take-home return for the mutual fund.

There are plenty of no-load funds that have had similar or better performance than load funds. Studies have not been able to prove that load funds have performed better than no-load funds. In fact, *Consumer Reports* conducted an analysis of Morningstar data that showed that load funds in the nine domestic-stock categories surveyed did not produce higher returns than no-load funds over the one-, three-, five-, or 10-year time periods.

When one buys a load fund instead of a comparable no-load fund, an investor is starting off with a 3 to 5 percent disadvantage. It takes tremendous performance for a load fund to make this up. Loads are there to give brokers an incentive to push a product—they are not in an investor's best interest. Furthermore, if an investor is doing the legwork of finding appropriate mutual funds, why pay a broker? If you want to support your broker, then invest in load funds. If you want to put more of your investment dollars to work for yourself, invest in no-load funds.

Expense Ratios

Investors have a choice as to whether to buy a load or a no-load fund. With other fees, you don't have a choice. All funds (load or no-load funds) have expense ratios. These costs vary from fund to fund. Expense ratios incorporate the costs of managing the fund, transaction costs, and administrative functions, such as shareholder mailings. Annual expenses are an excellent way to see a mutual fund's attitude toward its shareholders. If a fund has an outrageously high expense ratio, it probably doesn't have its shareholders best interests in mind.

Equity funds generally have higher expense ratios than fixed income funds; funds with international stocks tend to have higher expense ratios than funds with domestic equities; and funds that are actively managed tend to have higher expense ratios than funds that are designed to mirror an index. According to fund tracker Lipper Inc., the average expense ratio on mutual funds was 1.38 percent in 2003. Investors should try to avoid domestic equity funds that have expense ratios above 1.00 percent, fixed income funds with expense ratios above 0.75 percent, and international funds with expense ratios above 1.50 percent. Morningstar's database lists 467 funds that have expense ratios over 2 percent (*SmartMoney*, February 2005, page 62). Academics at the University of Minnesota and the University of West Florida studied fund performance over a 10-year period and found that each percentage point increase in expense ratio knocks 2 to 6 percent off total return (*SmartMoney*, February 2005, page 62). Investors who put money in no-load funds with low expense ratios will be starting off with a huge advantage over other, more expensive funds.

OTHER FACTORS

Turnover

Turnover of the securities within a mutual fund is another factor about which investors should be cognizant. Turnover is generally defined as the amount of time the average security is held in a mutual fund. High turnover translates into higher costs in a few different ways.

For example, the dollar value and number of buy and sell transactions can have a big affect on a fund's tax liabilities. High turnover usually results in higher tax requirements for fund holders. Since 2001, mutual funds have been required to provide after-tax returns to help investors understand the effect of taxes on returns.

Also, the more purchases and sales there are in a mutual fund, the more brokerage costs are incurred. In many cases, because mutual funds trade in large blocks they do not get the best available price. Turnover is a cost that is not as explicit as a load or an expense ratio, but it still can hurt an investor's overall return. Investors should try to stay clear of funds that have yearly turnover above 100 percent.

Performance

Another variable that mutual funds are often screened for is performance. In their advertising, mutual fund companies are nearly always touting their performance, especially of their best performers. On most screeners an investor can screen by performance numbers over various time periods. The CFA Institute requires money management firms to show a 10-year performance record (or a record for the period since inception, if it less than 10 years) to meet their performance presentation standards. They require annual returns to be presented and for performance less than one year not to be annualized.

Investors should not screen for performance for any period less than three years. Periods less than three years are too short a time span to make any kind of judgment on a fund. Ideally, an investor should evaluate a mutual fund's performance over a business cycle that incorporates bull and bear markets. Often, the best performing mutual funds for a given year underperform the following year. Funds that have consistently beaten their benchmark over long periods of time are the ones that should garner the most attention of investors.

A strong, consistent track record is certainly an attractive feature of any fund. It is important to see how funds have done in various investment climates because no one knows exactly what environment they will face going forward. Remember that when screening for performance, only past results are revealed. Future results can be very different from what happened in the past. In any marketing material and all commercials for mutual funds, there is always a statement that says something to the effect of, "Past performance is no guarantee of future results. Fund historical performance does not promise the same results in the future." Investors should remember these warnings before putting money in any mutual fund. An investor should not look at performance as an isolated factor, but should combine it with other variables in looking for good mutual funds.

Manager Tenure

If a fund has had wonderful performance in the past but the portfolio manager recently left the firm, an investor should think twice about putting money in the fund. It's not a judgment against the new portfolio manager, but the performance record for the mutual fund—which you have screened for and perhaps further researched—is not theirs. If you're going to use performance returns as one of the factors in selecting a mutual fund, make sure that the performance record was from the current portfolio manager.

Investors should want the portfolio manager to have at least five years of a performance record to judge. In professional portfolio management, there is a steep learning curve. Some rookie portfolio managers may do a splendid job managing some mutual funds, but picking them is merely guesswork. The same way one would not want to go to a surgeon performing his first operation, investors should not want their money managed by a rookie portfolio manager: *experience counts.*

A weakness of the manager tenure variable is that some mutual funds are managed by more than one individual. Some fund families believe in the group or team approach to running money, as opposed to mutual funds being managed by a "star" portfolio manager. On a screen, funds that are team managed will not show up as having any manager changes, even if there have been changes of members of the portfolio team, or if the job responsibilities of individuals in the team have changed.

Team managed funds have the advantage of using a variety of viewpoints. The disadvantage, though, is that ultimately, at the end of the day, one person has to make the buy and sell decisions for the portfolio. Whether a fund is managed by a single person or a team, it is generally a positive sign that the managers themselves have their own money invested in the fund. This assures that the managers and fund holders' interests are aligned. It also gives the portfolio manager an added incentive to do the best job he or she can possibly do in managing the fund.

Risk

Another variable that investment performance should be combined with is risk. If Mutual Fund A and Mutual Fund B both have had the same five-year return and the same investment style but Fund A has been much more volatile than Fund B, Fund B would appear to be the better investment choice. One goal of any investor should be to try to maximize return for any given level of risk.

Initial Investment

The initial investment requirement is an important factor to some investors. Most investors are limited in the amount of money they can put into a single mutual fund. Funds vary on the minimum amount required to open up an account. Some require as little as $250, and others require a minimum of $10,000. Funds with smaller opening requirements are generally geared toward individual investors, while those with larger asset requirements are geared more toward institutions. Funds with small initial requirements may require an investor to put in a certain additional amount each month to the fund. The only advantage that the funds with larger initial investment requirements provide is that in many cases they have slightly lower expense ratios.

Amount of Assets

The amount of assets in the fund is a secondary characteristic that may be worthy of screening. In terms of assets in an active fund, an investor generally wants to avoid funds with less than $100 million and those with more than $10 billion. Funds with small amounts of assets are more likely to shut down than larger funds. In the past three years, 14.8 percent of active domestic equity funds have liquidated or merged; in the past year, 6.6 percent of funds were liquidated or merged. It's likely that funds without a lot of assets will not to be as efficient and diversified as larger funds.

A problem with very large active funds is that sometimes they end up providing indexlike returns. They become overdiversified, making it difficult for the portfolio manager to make meaningful bets on specific sectors and securities. Investing large amounts of money makes it difficult to accumulate meaningful positions in individual securities without influencing their price, especially if these issues have relatively small capitalizations. It is also sometimes difficult for funds with large sums of money (especially small cap funds) to find many worthy investment candidates to invest in. Funds are often limited in the percentage of outstanding stock of a company that they can purchase. Taking large positions in a stock (especially ones with small market capitalizations) can hurt a fund's liquidity and make for inefficient trade executions.

Concentration Level

Investors should be aware of the concentration level of a fund. Although not a variable in many screeners, this information is released a few times a year by the fund company when it displays its holdings. Individual security posistions greater than five percent should be scrutinized. Investors should look at how many securities are in the mutual fund and the percentage of the top 10 positions in the fund. Funds that have less than 30 positions and/or the top 10 positions make up more than 40 percent of the portfolio are highly concentrated. High concentration is not necessarily a negative feature, but a mutual fund investor should know that these funds will have more risk and tend to have a higher tracking error (the variation of a security's return to a benchmark) than less concentrated funds.

LESS EASILY DISCERNED FACTORS

Investors should be aware that they are generally only able to see the actual holdings in a mutual fund at a specific point in time only a few times during the year. Mutual funds often change their holdings before the end of a quarter so that they do not have to show stocks on their statements that had significant down moves, and they can show stocks that have had large price increases. This process is sometimes referred to as window dressing because it doesn't show the true characteristics of the portfolio during the reporting period.

Over the past few years, the mutual fund industry has been put in a bad light by some illegal and unethical acts of some firms in the business.

The two acts that some firms were found to have engaged in were market timing and late trading of funds.

Market timing is an investment technique involving short-term in and out trading of mutual fund shares. It is designed to exploit the market inefficiency when the NAV of the mutual fund shares set at the market close does not reflect the current market value of the securities held by the mutual fund. This became prevalent for international funds whose funds were priced at one time while the actual securities were trading ahead of that time. Market timers realize a riskless profit when they buy mutual funds at the stale NAV and sell the shares the next day at the funds' true value.

Mutual fund companies state in their prospectuses that they discourage or prohibit this activity, but clearly some allowed it to occur. The buy and hold fund holders were the biggest victims of this kind of activity because it ended up hurting the overall return of the fund. Mutual funds were not intended to be trading vehicles. To try to combat market timing, more money management firms have begun to issue large redemption fees for investors who redeem soon after buying shares of a mutual fund.

Late trading or "after hours trading" involves placing orders for mutual funds shares after the 4:00 P.M. close but still getting that day's closing price, rather than the next day's closing price. This practice is illegal under SEC rules, but some managers allowed exceptions for some large clients such as hedge funds and wealthy individuals. By late trading, investors could take advantage of news reported after the closing bell which was not reflected in the mutual fund's price. New York Attorney General Eliot Spitzer likened late-day trading to "betting on yesterday's horse races." Funds that allowed this kind of activity by some select fund holders, besides doing something illegal, damaged the returns of other fund holders who did not engage in this activity.

Of course, these illegal and unethical actions were not engaged in by every firm in the industry. A large group of mutual fund firms, including Vanguard and T. Rowe Price, have not been found to have participated in any of these types of activities. Investors should not shy away from mutual funds because of the action of a few. By the same token, they should try to invest with a firm with high ethics and whose philosophy and actions reflect that the customer comes first. Honesty and integrity are important. Why put your money with any firm that does not uphold the highest standards?

EXAMPLES OF FUND SCREENS

The examples of mutual fund screens in this section were run in the first quarter of 2005. They should be used as ideas on how to find mutual funds that may be worthy of further research. All the funds screened for have no loads and a minimum of $100 million in assets. Investors should be aware that if they run the same screen, the mutual funds returned may be different because of time disparities.

Large Cap Value Mutual Funds

The screen in Figure 11-7 looks for attractive mutual funds with the large cap value investment style. They all are low cost, being no-load and with an expense ratio no greater than 1 percent. The funds have all had good historical risk/return performance, which is shown by the Standard & Poor's five-star ranking. Each of the portfolio managers has been managing their respective mutual fund since at least 1998. Investors should be aware that some of the funds returned by the screen are team managed. Mutual funds combining strong returns, low cost, and experienced managers are worthy candidates for further research by investors seeking a large cap value mutual fund.

Small Cap Growth Mutual Funds

The screen in Figure 11-8 searches for appealing mutual funds with the small cap growth style. They're all no-load and with an expense ratio no greater than 1 percent. The search criteria specified a portfolio manager start date no later than 1999, and the funds produced by this screen have had the same portfolio manager since at least 1997. All funds have at least a four-star ranking from Standard & Poor's, and each has assets between $100 million and $9 billion. For investors looking to invest in a small cap growth fund, these funds are worth further inspection.

General Equity Funds with Low Risk and
Strong Return Characteristics

The equity funds filtered by the screen in Figure 11-9 have the rare and desirable traits of great historical returns combined with low historical risk. Each has a five-star ranking and a low risk ranking from

FIGURE 11-7 Large cap value funds.

*Search Criteria	Low Value	High Value
U.S. Markets		
Large Cap Value		
Portfolio Manager Start Date		1998
Assets (Millions)	$100	
Expense Ratio		1.00%
S&P Stars Ranking	5	

Output

Symbol	Mutual Fund	Portfolio Manager Start Date	Assets (Millions)	Expense Ratio	Stars Ranking	Portfolio Manager
AAGAX	Amer Aadvantage Large Cap Value AMR	Aug. 94	777	0.39%	5	William Quinn/Nancy Eck
DFLVX	DFA US Large Cap Value	Feb. 93	2,628	0.30%	5	Robert Deere
DFCVX	DFA US Large Cap Value II	Aug. 94	196	0.22%	5	Team Managed
DODGX	Dodge & Cox Stock	Jan. 65	41,436	0.54%	5	Team Managed
UMBIX	Excelsior Value & Restructuring	Dec. 92	4,115	0.99%	5	David Williams
LEXCX	ING Corporate Leaders Trust Series B A	Nov. 98	305	0.59%	5	Team Managed
TALVX	Target Large Cap Value	Jan. 93	381	0.80%	5	B Kroll/N Buziak

*Screen was run on Kiplinger.com.

169

FIGURE 11-8 Small cap growth funds.

*Search Criteria	Low Value	High Value
U.S. Markets		
Small Cap Growth		
Portfolio Manager Start Date		1999
Assets (Millions)	$100	$8,000
Expense Ratio		1.00%
S&P Stars Ranking	4	

Output

Symbol	Mutual Fund	Assets (Millions)	Expense Ratio	Stars Ranking	Portfolio Manager Start Date	Portfolio Manager
VEXRX	BlackRock Small Cap Growth Equity	301	0.89%	4	Sep. 93	N Wagner/B Stack
JAVTX	Janus Venture	1,411	0.93%	4	Feb. 97	William Bales
MERDX	Meridian Growth	1,632	0.88%	4	Aug. 84	Richard Aster
HIASX	Nicholas Limited Edition	154	0.91%	4	Mar. 93	David Nicholas
OGGFX	One Group Small Cap Growth	636	0.99%	4	May. 96	Team Managed
PRNHX	T. Rowe Price New Horizons	5,565	0.91%	4	Jan. 88	J Laporte/Team Managed

*Screen was run on Kiplinger.com.

FIGURE 11-9 General equity funds with strong risk and return characteristics.

*Search Criteria

	Low Value	High Value
U.S. Equity Minimum Initial Investment Amount		$2,500 or less
Morningstar Rating	5 Stars	5 Stars
Morningstar Risk	Low	Low
Expense Ratio		1.00%

Output

Symbol	Mutual Fund	Morningstar Rating	Morningstar Risk	3-Year Return	5-Year Return
TWEIX	American Century Equity Income	5	Low	9.74%	12.44%
FCNTX	Fidelity Contrafund	5	Low	9.69%	0.97%
FVALX	Forester Value	5	Low	9.19%	7.21%
PRBLX	Parnassus Equity Income	5	Low	5.26%	6.26%
TRSGX	T. Rowe Price Personal Strat Grwth	5	Low	8.67%	4.76%

*Screen was run on mfea.com.

171

Morningstar. They have low expenses, as illustrated by an expense ratio of no more than 1 percent. The funds are also attractive to individual investors because they only require $2,500 or less to open. Some high performing mutual funds require more than $10,000 to open, which pretty much prevents the average investor from owning them. Funds that pass the filters set in this screen should certainly garner interest to investors looking for equity exposure.

Select European Equity Mutual Funds

The screen on Figure 11-10 displays mutual funds holding European stocks. Most of the economies in this region are fairly developed. The expense ratio allowed is widened to 1.50 percent because of the higher costs in running a fund holding foreign stocks. The funds also need to have assets of at least $100 million and a minimum ranking of three stars from Standard & Poor's. The funds returned by the screen are worth consideration for investment for someone seeking to diversify their assets with some European equity exposure.

Attractive Short-Term Taxable Bond Funds

The screen in Figure 11-11 looks for short-term taxable bond funds with at least a four-star ranking from Standard & Poor's. Like the other mutual fund screens, each fund has at least $100 million in assets and is no-load. The funds are screened for expense ratios of no more than 1 percent, and they must have the same portfolio manager since 1999. There are also filters appropriate for fixed income funds. Each of the funds has an average bond rating of AAA from Standard & Poor's and an average maturity of less than five years. Investors looking for safe and inexpensive short-term fixed income funds should consider the funds returned by this screen.

Exchange-Traded Funds

Despite offering many benefits, mutual funds do have some weaknesses. The two main weaknesses are that they are priced only once daily and that their holdings and expenses are not transparent. The fact that they are priced only once daily was the main reason that the late trading and market timing problems could occur with some funds. If mutu-

FIGURE 11-10 European equity funds.

*Search Criteria	Low Value	High Value
International Equities		
Regional		
European Equity		
Assets (Millions)	$100	
Expense Ratio		1.50%
S&P Stars Ranking	3	

Output

Symbol	Mutual Fund	Assets (Millions)	Expense Ratio	Stars Ranking	Portfolio Manager
FECAX	Fidelity Europe Capital Appreciation	457	1.32%	3	Ian Hart
FNORX	Fidelity Nordic	158	1.40%	3	Trygue Toraasen
MEURX	Mutual European Z	650	1.08%	4	Matthew Haynes/David Winters
PRESX	T. Rowe Price European Stock	823	1.12%	3	Team Managed
VEURX	Vanguard European Stock Index	9,220	0.32%	3	Team Managed
VESIX	Vanguard European Stock Index Instl	1,325	0.17%	3	Team Managed

*Screen was run on Kiplinger.com.

FIGURE 11-11   Short-term taxable bond funds.

*Search Criteria	Low Value	High Value
Short-Term Taxable Bonds		
S&P Stars Ranking	45	5
Assets (Millions)	$100	
Expense Ratio		1.00%
S&P Credit Rating	AAA	AAA
Average Maturity		5 years
Portfolio Manager Since		1999

Output

Symbol	Mutual Fund	S&P Stars Ranking	Assets (Millions)	Expense Ratio
APSTX	American Performance Short Term Income	5	256	0.52%
CLDBX	BlackRock Low Duration	4	760	0.40%
RFBSX	F Russell Short Duration Bond S	4	1,154	0.56%
HLLVX	One Group Short Term Bond I	4	1,078	0.55%
ONUAX	One Group Ultra Short Term Bond A	4	311	0.70%
HLGFX	One Group Ultra Short Term Bond 1	4	1,213	0.45%
PLDAX	Pimco Low Duration Admin	5	420	0.68%
PTLAX	PIMCO Low Duration A	4	2,009	0.90%
PLDDX	Pimco Low Duration D	5	702	0.75%
PTLDX	PIMCO Low Duration Instl	5	9,550	0.43%

Symbol	S&P Credit Rating	Average Maturity	Portfolio Manager Since
APSTX	AAA	2.55	Oct. 94
CLDBX	AAA	2.00	Jun. 97
RFBSX	AAA	1.90	Jan. 95
HLLVX	AAA	1.80	May 93
ONUAX	AAA	2.74	May 93
HLGFX	AAA	2.74	May 93
PLDAX	AAA	1.83	Jan. 95
PTLAX	AAA	1.83	Jan. 97
PLDDX	AAA	1.83	Apr. 98
PTLDX	AAA	1.83	May 87

*Screen was run on Kiplinger.com.

al funds were priced continuously throughout the trading day, these unethical and illegal acts would most likely never have had the opportunity to take place.

The other main flaw is that when an investor buys a mutual fund, it is not always clear exactly what he or she is buying and what the cost is.

Mutual funds only have to publicly declare what their holdings are a couple of times a year. As previously stated, some funds window-dress their positions at the end of the quarter by purchasing top performing stocks and selling underperforming stocks to give the appearance that the fund had different characteristics than it actually did for most of the reporting quarter. A fund that reports its holdings more than required and keeps fund holders abreast of its actions on a regular basis would be viewed very positively by many investors. Unfortunately, this kind of clear communication rarely takes place.

Mutual funds also fail to adequately describe their allocation fees, and it's unclear what specific fees and what amounts get rolled up into an expense ratio. If investors clearly saw how much they were actually paying in expenses for their mutual funds, they would no doubt be unpleasantly surprised.

Advantages of ETFs

An investment product that solves many of these weaknesses is exchange-traded funds. These investments have attracted a lot of assets over the past 10 years. As of August 30, 2004, there were 143 ETFs with assets of $174.51 billion, up 49 percent from one year earlier, according to the Investment Company Institute. In the same period, assets of mutual funds rose 7.1 percent. Examples of exchange-traded funds such as Standard & Poor's Spiders (SPX), the Nasdaq 100 Tracking Stock (QQQ), and the Dow Industrial Diamonds (DIA) are three of the most highly traded securities. In the coming years, ETFs are going to become even more popular as an investment choice of individuals and institutions.

The variety of exchange-traded funds offerings is expanding. They are not just based on the major market indices anymore. There are equity ETFs geared toward specific sectors of the market, countries and geographic regions, and investment styles. Within the last year, ETFs have been introduced that are invested in Chinese companies, and others that are tied to the price of gold. In the fixed income area, although there are not as many offerings as the equities investment class, there are ETFs with short- and long-term maturities and ETFs with various classifications of bonds.

Exchange-traded funds are a package of securities based on an index, rolled up into one security that is traded like a stock throughout the day on one of the major stock exchanges. Presently, they are basically a combination of an index fund and a stock. They are regulated by the Securities and Exchange Commission, and to date, according to etfzone .com, no U.S. investor has ever lost money due to fraudulent ETFs. There are three main structures for ETFs:

- Open-ended mutual funds
- Unit investment trusts
- Exchange-traded grantor trusts

The *open-ended mutual fund structure* is the most popular. Funds with this structure are registered with the SEC and can reinvest the dividends they receive from the underlying securities in the fund when they receive them. The open-end structure allows a fund to use stock index futures, which enables the fund to have extremely low tracking error from the benchmarked index. ETFs with this structure can participate in security lending. The money generated from these loans can contribute to lower expenses. Examples of ETFs with the open-end mutual fund structure include VIPERs, iShares, and Select Sector SPDR funds.

The *unit investment trust structure* is the way the first ETFs were structured, such as the SPDRs and Diamonds. ETFs with this structure accumulate dividends on their underlying securities and reinvest them quarterly, causing a cash drag. Funds with this structure are also regulated by the SEC.

Exchange-traded grantor trusts operate a little differently from the other structures. These funds do not track a specific index. The securities included in the fund are determined by the fund provider or an independent investment advisor. They generally have either a specific investment style or are in a certain sector. Once the fund is created, its security composition does not change unless there is a corporate action such as a merger. This means that over time the weighting of the securities in the ETF can change significantly based on their individual performances. Also, with grantor trusts, an investor is allowed to take physical delivery of the underlying securities in the fund. Merrill Lynch's HOLDRS are an example of ETFs with the exchange-traded grantor structure.

ETFs offer many advantages compared to mutual funds. They are generally cheaper and more tax efficient than active and indexed mutual funds. ETFs have no 12b-1 fees. The average expense ratio for ETFs is

0.46 percent , while the average for index equity mutual funds is 0.68 percent (*Standard & Poor's Outlook,* February 11, 2004). Differences between ETF fees and actively managed mutual funds are typically 1 percent per year, which compounded over the long term results in a considerable return discrepancy. Overall, with ETFs less of an investor's profits are taken by middlemen. The only two expenses an ETF investor has are the expense ratio of the fund and the commission paid to a broker to buy or sell the security. In today's highly competitive financial markets, many discount brokers offer commissions of less than $20 a trade. The tax advantage of ETFs stems from much lower turnover, especially compared to active mutual funds. With low turnover, they rarely make capital gains distributions, so no tax is due on any gains until you actually sell the security.

Unlike mutual funds, which are priced once a day, ETFs are traded throughout the day. The continuous trading eliminates the chance of late trading and market timing by investors. Many investors perceive ETFs as providing a more level playing field than mutual funds. They offer the added flexibility of the ability to be bought on margin or shorted, for investors who want to make aggressive bets or use defensive strategies in their overall portfolios. They can also be purchased or sold using limit and stop orders, which allows investors to better specify the price at which they are willing to trade their shares.

Exchange-traded funds are fully invested and more efficient than mutual funds. They do not have cash positions. Mutual fund managers need to have a portion of their portfolio in cash to meet redemptions. Also, when they receive inflows it often takes them some time to invest into actual securities, causing them to have cash positions. This cash position that a mutual fund manager needs to keep is sometimes referred to as a "cash drag" because in a bull market the cash position hurts a mutual fund's total return. Stocks significantly outperform cash in bull markets.

Drawbacks of ETFs

Exchange-traded funds have very few negatives. One weakness, however, is that thinly traded funds, such as certain sector and country funds, may have high bid-ask spreads of 30 cents or more. The ETFs that are widely traded have a low bid-ask spread resembling large blue chip stocks. Another negative is that ETFs are not well suited for dollar-cost averaging. For investors to add a specific dollar amount to an ETF every period would result in a lot of commissions going to the broker or financial advisor placing the trades. Finally, securities or markets that are illiquid are not appropriate for ETFs. Continuous pricing of securities such as some junk bonds and small cap emerging market stocks does not exist. It is imperative for securities in ETFs to be priced fairly consistently for a fund to be viable.

All exchange-traded funds are based on indexes or portfolios where the securities do not change. There are no active ETFs. Structuring active ETFs has been met with legal and trading concerns from the regulatory authorities. There is a concern that the transparency of the portfolios may be compromised and that traders would be able to front-run the trades of ETF managers. Despite these concerns, active ETFs, in some form, will likely be offered in the near future with some modifications. There have been applications to the SEC for such funds, but to date none has been successful.

Screening for ETFs

Currently, it is difficult to screen exclusively for exchange-traded funds. Two main features an investor should look at in picking ETFs are its expense ratio and how well it has mirrored its index. In the future, as ETFs grow in popularity, there will probably be multiple Web sites where a potential investor will be able to screen for them. Figure 11-12 on pages 180–181 shows a sample of various ETFs and some of the characteristics that will be available on screens in the future.

POINTS TO REMEMBER

▶ When screening for mutual funds, an investor should take the following steps:

1. Determine your investment goals and objectives
2. Determine what kind of mutual funds can best satisfy your needs
3. Determine what mutual fund characteristics are important to you
4. Put in parameters for variables and run the screen

5. Select mutual funds to purchase
6. Follow up and see how the fund has performed and whether it is satisfying your goals

▶ Mutual funds have become increasingly popular over the past 10 years.

▶ Some of the main benefits of mutual funds are diversification at a low cost, convenience, and professional management.

▶ Cost, portfolio manager tenure, and past performance over long time periods are factors that should be stressed when screening for mutual funds.

▶ Knowledgeable investors should never pay a sales load for a mutual fund.

▶ Exchange-traded funds rectify many of the weaknesses of mutual funds.

▶ When examining ETFs, an investor should focus on its expense ratio and tracking error to its targeted index.

FIGURE 11-12   Examples of exchange-traded funds.

Name	Ticker	Inception Date	Market Return 1yr %	Expense Ratio	ETF Structure	Index Tracked
Broad Based/Large Cap						
DIAMONDS Trust Series I	DIA	1/20/1998	18.63	0.18	Unit investment trust	Dow Jones Industrial Average
SPDR Trust Series I	SPY	1/29/1993	18.89	0.10	Unit investment trust	S&P 500 Index
NASDAQ-100 Index Tracking Stock	QQQ	3/10/1999	26.19	0.20	Unit investment trust	NASDAQ 100 Index
iShares Russell 3000 Index Fund	IWV	5/22/2000	20.21	0.20	Open-end mutual fund	Russell 3000
Broad Based/ Mid Cap						
iShares S&P MidCap 400 Index Fund	IJH	7/17/2001	27.59	0.20	Open-end mutual fund	S&P MidCap 400 Index
MidCap SPDR Trust Series I	MDY	5/4/1995	27.79	0.25	Unit investment trust	S&P MidCap 400 Index
Vanguard Mid-Cap VIPERS	VO	1/26/2004	na	0.18	Open-end mutual fund	MSCI U.S. Mid Cap 450 Index
Broad Based/ Small Cap						
iShares S&P SmallCap 600 Index Fund	IJR	5/22/2000	35.13	0.20	Open-end mutual fund	S&P SmallCap 600 Index
iShares Russell 2000 Index Fund	IWM	5/22/2000	34.39	0.20	Open-end mutual fund	Russell 2000 Index
iShares Morningstar Small Core Index Fund	JKJ	6/28/2004	na	0.25	Open-end mutual fund	Morningstar Small Core Index
Sector						
Merrill Lynch Retail HOLDRS	RTH	5/2/2001	na	0.08	Grantor trust	No independent index
Select Sector SPDR Fund-Energy	XLE	12/22/1998	32.13	0.28	Open-end mutual fund	Energy Select Sector Index
Vanguard Financial VIPERs	VFH	1/26/2004	na	0.28	Open-end mutual fund	MSCI U.S. Investable Market Financials Index
iShares Dow Jones U.S. Healthcare Sector Index Fund	IYH	6/12/2000	8.75	0.60	Open-end mutual fund	Dow Jones U.S. healthcare Sector Index
iShares Cohen&Steers Realty Majors Index Fund	ICF	1/29/2001	28.57	0.35	Open-end mutual fund	Cohen & Steers Realty Majors Index
Select Sector SPDR Fund-Technology	XLK	12/22/1998	21.27	0.28	Open-end mutual fund	Technology Select Sector Index

(Continued)

FIGURE 11-12 *Continued.*

Name	Ticker	Inception Date	Market Return 1yr %	Expense Ratio	ETF Structure	Index Tracked
			Foreign/Global			
iShares S&P Global 100 Index Fund	IOO	12/5/2000	20.62	0.40	Open-end mutual fund	S&P Global 100 Index
Merrill Lynch Market 2000+ HOLDRS	MKH	8/30/2000	na	0.08	Grantor trust	No independent index
			Foreign/Country			
iShares MSCI-Germany	EWG	3/12/1996	35.57	0.59	Open-end mutual fund	MSCI Germany Index
iShares MSCI-Hong Kong	EWH	3/12/1996	34.65	0.59	Open-end mutual fund	MSCI Hong Kong-Index
iShares MSCI-United Kingdom	EWU	3/12/1996	25.62	0.59	Open-end mutual fund	MSCI-United Kingdom Index
			Foreign/Sector			
iShares S&P Global Financial Index Fund	IXG	11/12/2001	23.82	0.65	Open-end mutual fund	S&P Global Financials Sector Index
iShares S&P Global Info Technology Index Fund	IXN	11/12/2001	26.29	0.65	Open-end mutual fund	S&P Global Info Technology Sector Index

12

SCREENING FOR BONDS

The people who sustain the worst losses are usually those who overreach. And it's not necessary: Steady, moderate gains will get you where you want to go.

—John Train

SCREENING FOR INDIVIDUAL bonds is not nearly as widely available as screening for individual stocks or mutual funds. There are much fewer Web sites that have screeners for separate fixed income securities. Still, bonds are part of most individual and institutional portfolios. Screening provides a helpful way to find appropriate individual bonds to invest in based on the characteristics an investor is looking for in these securities.

Bonds are IOUs issued by corporations and governments. They are loans, not ownership positions like stocks. Bonds serve as a way for these entities to borrow money to finance their economic activity. Most bonds pay the holder the amount borrowed (principal) at a designated future date plus a fixed amount of interest in regular intervals, which comes in the form of coupons.

Investors are drawn to bonds for four main reasons:

1. Diversification
2. Income

3. Total return

4. Special circumstances

Fixed income securities provide diversification to portfolios mainly composed of equity positions. Bonds do not move in lockstep with stocks. Certain factors affect fixed income securities differently than equities. The process of spreading money among different types of investments helps reduce your exposure to risk.

As a rule of thumb, bond investors are more focused on the asset and liability makeup of the balance sheet, while equity investors are more concerned with activities on the income statement. The level and changes in interest rates and inflation have historically had a bigger proportional impact on bond prices than equity prices.

Many investors put money in bonds because of the income they produce on a regular basis. Coupons on highly rated bonds are much more predictable and stable than dividend distributions on stocks. Conservative investors are attracted to highly rated bonds because of the safety of the income. For many individuals, the coupons serve as a supplement for earned income and government benefits such as Social Security payments.

Investors sometimes underestimate the return potential of fixed income securities. In many time periods of less than five years, bonds have outperformed stocks. Over long time periods, however, equities have outperformed. Going back 25 years, there is no rolling 10-year period in which bonds have outperformed stocks. The long-term average annual return for bonds is 8.9 percent, compared to 12.3 percent for the stock market (the 30-year returns through December 31, 2003, for the Lehman Brothers Government/Credit Index and the Dow Jones Wilshire 5000 Composite Index, respectively). However, bonds offer these historic returns with much lower risk levels than equities.

Looking into the near future, there is no guarantee that equities will outperform fixed income. The more uncertainty and nervousness in the overall economy there is going forward, the more attractive fixed income investments—especially short-term maturities and high quality issues—are to many investors. In times of crisis there is almost always a strong demand for these types of bonds.

Government bonds and corporate bonds with high debt ratings offer steady income and much lower volatility than equities. If a company goes bankrupt, bondholders have a higher claim to the firm's assets than stock-holders. It is better to be a bondholder than a stockholder of a company if it goes bust. In nearly every individual and institutional asset mix, there is a strong argument that could be made for some kind of fixed income component to be included.

There are specific types of bonds that can help investors with certain needs or concerns. For example, the interest on most municipal bonds is not subject to state and federal income taxes if the bonds are purchased by a resident of the issuing state. These can be appropriate holdings for investors in high tax brackets or those who live in high income tax areas. Investors concerned about inflation can invest in Treasury Inflation-Protected Securities (TIPS), which provide a degree of inflation protection. For those who need a specific amount of money at a specific point in time in the future (asset-liability matching), zero coupon bonds are very attractive. Insurance companies often use bonds to try to match their assets with their liabilities.

There are bonds with different risk profiles. High yield (junk) bonds have a high risk of default, while Treasury bonds have virtually no risk of not making their principal and interest payments. Generally, the higher the risk, the higher the coupon rate and total return possibilities. As has been stated before, in order to get outsized returns, one has to take on more risk and choose securities that outperform their benchmark.

RISKS BOND INVESTORS FACE

Fixed income securities face some of the same risks as equities such as inflation and liquidity risk. Bonds also come with some of their own specific types of risk. For example, *default risk* is the risk that the bond issuer delays or does not repay its interest and principal obligations. Credit ratings try to quantify this type of risk for specific bond issues. Credit ratings incorporate such items as interest coverage, debt levels, and cash positions into one specific rating. Figure 12-1 shows Standard & Poor's bond rating categories.

Bond issues with higher credit ratings have a lower chance of defaulting on their debt. The greatest default rate in the United States occurred during the Great Depression in the 1930s. In 1932 the default rate for corporate bonds reached 9.2 percent (*Moody's Investor Services Global*

FIGURE 12-1   Standard & Poor's bond rating categories.

Investment Grade Bonds

AAA	Highest Quality
AA	High Quality
A	High Medium-Grade
BBB	Medium-Grade

High-Yield or Junk Bonds

BB	Uncertain Outlook
B	Generally Lacking Desirable Qualities
CCC	Poor Quality, Danger of Default
CCC	Very Speculative, May Be in Default
D	In Default

Credit Research, Special Comment, "Historical Default Rates of Corporate Bond Issues, 1920–1999," January 2000).

Issuers face *credit risk* in regard to the movement up or down of their debt rating. If a bond is downgraded it means that the company will need to borrow funds at higher rates, which can end up costing a corporation or municipal government body millions of dollars over time. Bondholders owning issues that are downgraded will see a decline in their price.

Credit spread risk is the risk that the interest rate difference for a risky bond over a risk-free bond will increase after the risky bond has been purchased. Corporate bonds are typically priced at a spread to comparable U.S. Treasury bonds, which are generally considered risk-free. If the spread widens after purchase of the risky bond, its price will decline. Spreads can widen based on activities in the overall U.S. economy such as GDP growth, the inflation rate, and employment levels.

Interest rate risk is concerned with the effects of moves in interest rates on bond prices. Simply put, upward moves in interest rates hurt bond prices, while downward moves in interest rates help bond prices. Longer maturity bonds face greater interest rate risk. A longer time to maturity equals greater uncertainty of what might happen in the future. This is what one sees most of the time with the yield curve. Generally, the yield curve is upward sloping, which means yields get higher the longer the maturity of a bond. If an investor has to sell a bond before its maturity date, an increase in interest rates will result in a capital loss. Investors should be aware that it is possible that a short-term bond will return more than a long-term bond when interest rates are rising.

Some bonds face *call risk*. Bonds that have provisions whereby they can be repaid before maturity are considered "callable." Those that cannot be redeemed by the issuer before their maturity date are "noncallable." If interest rates drop significantly, bond issuers may be tempted to call their bonds. The risk to investors if a bond is called is that they face reinvesting their proceeds at lower interest rates that would not be as desirable as from those of the old bond. Also, an investor in callable bonds can never be certain of the schedule of its cash flow, while knowing that the capital appreciation is pretty much limited to the callable price. Investors are generally paid for taking call risk by means of a discounted price or a higher yield. It is not easy to determine if this compensation is sufficient.

Finally, some government agency bonds face *prepayment risk*. If interest rates fall, there is an incentive for borrowers to prepay their loans and mortgages or to refinance. As higher rate loans disappear, the agency bonds must reinvest their assets in lower yielding loans, which hurts their overall return.

When screening for fixed income securities, the first major decision an investor must make is what type of bond to invest in. This decision should not be taken lightly by investors, because different bond types offer very different risk and return profiles. All bonds are not created equal. With individual common stocks there are only two types of instrument to invest in: "common stock" and "preferred stock." Preferred share owners have a higher claim to a firm's remaining assets if there is a bankruptcy, and preferred shares generally offer higher yields than common shares. With individual fixed income issues, there are several types of instruments in which you can place your money. Individuals should have a solid idea of the purpose of their fixed income position in their portfolio before starting to screen for bonds. At a minimum they should know if they're looking for short- or long-term bonds, taxable or nontaxable issues, and/or investment-grade-rated or junk-rated bonds.

Figure 12-2 is an example of a bond screener.

FIGURE 12-2   Sample bond screener.

Filters

Bond Type

	min	max
Current Yield	min	max
Coupon	min	max
Yield to Maturity	min	max
Credit Rating	min	max
Average Maturity	min	max
Callable	yes	no

Search Now

SCREENING VARIABLES FOR BONDS

Bond screeners have fewer filters than equity screeners. All bond screeners have a filter for Bond Type, as can be seen in Figure 12-2. The main choices an investor has are Treasury, corporate, or municipal bonds. Within each of these broad bond categories there is a wide gamut of fixed income securities an investor can select.

Treasury and Agency Bonds

Treasury bonds are issued by the federal government. These securities are sold in order to pay off maturing debt and raise the cash needed to run the federal government. They are backed by the full faith and credit of the U.S. government. Rarely do Treasury bonds offer the best returns in the fixed income universe. However, they come with virtually no risk of not being able to make their interest and principal payments. There is only a minuscule probability that the government will not honor its debt. Even if the government is faced with difficult economic times where there are ballooning trade and budget deficits and massive unemployment, the government has always had the power to print money. The income earned on Treasury bonds is exempt from state and local taxes.

Treasury bonds are long-term obligations, with a term of more than 10 years. Treasury notes and Treasury bills are shorter-term obligations. Treasury notes have a term between one and 10 years, while Treasury bills mature in one year or less. Treasury issues pay interest twice a year and are very liquid—you can sell them at any time using a broker or directly through the U.S. Treasury.

Agency bonds are a spin-off from Treasury bonds. They are issued by government-sponsored entities such as the Federal National Mortgage Association (Fannie Mae), the Federal Home Loan Mortgage Corporation (Freddie Mac), the Government Mortgage Association (Ginnie Mae), and the Student Loan Marketing Association (Sallie Mae). These bonds are not officially backed by the federal government, but there is an implied backing. It is clearly not in the government's best interest to have these agencies fail. Agency bonds provide support to sectors of the economy that might otherwise find it difficult to find inexpensive sources of financing, such as low-income housing and loans for students. These bonds offer low risk because of their government affiliation, and higher returns than traditional Treasury bonds. The negative is that the minimum investment requirement for individual issues of these bonds can be more than $25,000

As mentioned earlier in the chapter, TIPS are another special type of Treasury bond. The principal of these bonds is tied to the inflation rate. Treasury Inflation Protected Securities are attractive to individuals who fear the effect sharp rises in inflation can have on the purchasing power of bonds. They are issued in five-, 10-, and 20-year maturities, in denominations and multiples of $1,000. These securities bear a stated interest rate and pay out semiannual interest payments. TIPS pay a small coupon each year, and their principal value is adjusted once a year to match the Consumer Price Index. The inflation adjustment counts as income in the year it is made. TIPS can be bought directly from the Treasury or as part of a mutual fund or an exchange-traded fund.

Another inflation-indexed Treasury security is the inflation-protected U.S. Savings Bond (I-Bond). The return on these bonds is based on a fixed rate that lasts up to 30 years and a rate that is based on inflation, which is adjusted every six months. These bonds can be bought through banks, not security brokers, in denominations from $50 to $10,000. I-Bonds have the added benefit of being exempt from state and local taxes and are not federally taxable until they are redeemed.

Corporate Bonds

Corporate bonds, as their name suggests, are issued by corporations. Companies use the money they collect from these bonds for various business purposes, such as expansion plans and asset purchases. Corporate bonds are riskier than Treasury and municipal bonds because they are not guaranteed by the government. Unlike Treasuries and municipal bonds, the earnings for corporate bonds are fully taxable. Their ability to pay back their bondholders is determined by the activities and financial status of the issuing company. These bonds are exposed to the unsystematic (nondiversifiable) risk of the individual issue. With the higher risk characteristic, they also offer the highest return potential.

Corporate bonds are the most diverse of any of the bond types. They come in short-term, intermediate, and long-term maturities. Some are convertible into common stock if certain conditions are met. Usually, the number of shares for which a convertible bond can be exchanged is fixed and the conversion privilege lasts for the life of the bond. Convertibles trade like equities when the stock price is high, like a bond when the stock price is low, and as a hybrid security when the stock is between these two cases. Some corporate bonds offer a floating rate of interest instead of the fixed rate offered by the majority of bonds. The interest rate paid on floating rate bonds moves with the rates on an index, like that of the short-term Treasury bill. These bonds provide protection against upward interest rate moves but usually offer a lower yield than fixed-rate corporate bonds with similar maturities.

Standard & Poor's and Moody's assign credit ratings to corporate bonds. These ratings help investors determine a company's ability to repay its debt and make its interest payments. Companies with stronger financial positions are given high credit ratings, while those with high levels of debt and low levels of liquidity are given lower credit ratings. Since the low-rated bonds have higher risk, they generally offer a higher coupon and greater return potential. The returns on lower rated bonds correlate more closely with equities than with highly rated fixed income securities. There is more of a chance that lower rated bonds will default on their debt obligations compared to higher rated issues. Corporations try to keep their credit rating high because the difference between an AAA rating and a junk status rating can mean millions of dollars in extra interest they have to pay.

Corporate bonds have some negative traits. Minimum investment requirements are high and accessible price histories are spotty for many individual corporate issues. Also, most professional portfolio managers and traders have expensive quantitative programs for evaluating corporate bonds features such as credit rating, call options, and time to maturity, which gives them an advantage over individual investors.

Municipal Bonds

Municipal bonds are issued by state and local governments. They are used to finance activities such as the construction of bridges, highway projects, and the building of dormitories at state universities. Municipal bonds are generally broken down into two types: General Obligation and Revenue bonds. General Obligation bonds are secured by the taxing and borrowing power of the issuing municipality, while Revenue bonds are secured by revenue from a specific municipal project.

Municipal bonds have slightly more risk than Treasuries. The amount of risk depends on the financial condition of the municipality. Like corporate bonds, they have debt ratings. Many municipal issues also have third party insurance, which makes them very unlikely to default. The main attraction of these bonds to investors is that they are exempt in most cases from city, state, and federal taxes.

If you buy a municipal bond issued by the state where you live, you don't have to pay federal and state income taxes on the interest that is paid on the bond. Even better, if you buy a municipal bond issue of the city or township where you live, in addition to not having to pay federal and state income taxes, you don't have to pay local income taxes on the interest of the bond. "Munis" generally offer a lower coupon rate than equivalent taxable bonds because of their triple tax-free status.

Recently, the average top-rated 10-year muni, as measured by the Lehman 10-year AAA muni index, yielded 3.8 percent, or about 90 percent, of the Treasury yield (*Standard & Poor's Outlook*, December 15, 2004). This type of yield disparity is most attractive for individuals in high tax brackets or high tax areas. Due to their tax-free status, many wealthy investors and individuals in geographic regions with high income tax levels have a portion of their assets in municipal bonds. To invest in individual municipal bonds requires a lot of money. A round lot of any particular issues requires as much as $250,000. Most financial planners feel $100,000 is the smallest amount that can be invested somewhat efficiently in individual municipal bonds. Individual investors often invest in municipal bonds through mutual funds because they require much lower dollar requirements, they have the diversification of many bond issues, and they offer professional portfolio management.

Another specialized type of bond is the zero coupon bond. These can be in the form of corporate bonds, municipals bonds, or Treasury bonds. These bonds, which began trading in the early 1980s, do not make interest payments. Instead, they are sold at large discounts to their face value, and at maturity the bondholder collects the principal plus all of the compounded interest. "Zeros" are most appropriate for investors looking for a set payout on a given date in the future. The drawback to these bonds is that holders are required to pay taxes each year on the interest as it is accruing. This sets up the negative situation of paying tax on money before it's actually received.

OTHER FACTORS TO CONSIDER

Bond Mutual Fund or Individual Bond Issue?

After deciding which type of bond best fits your circumstances, you need to determine in which form you're going to purchase the bond: as a mutual fund or an individual issue. Both methods have their pluses and minuses. Bond mutual funds and exchange-traded funds offer the diversification of owning many individual issues in one security. If one bond defaults or declines substantially in value in the fund, it will probably only have a minimum affect on the fund value. Bond funds and exchange-traded funds are convenient and easy to invest in and do not require large minimum investments. They also have professional portfolio managers overseeing the fund whose expertise is the fixed income market.

The negative of bond funds is that you don't own an individual bond. In fact, a bond fund does not have a specific date when you will get the principal back or pay a specific amount of interest each year. They are not suited for meeting specific obligations in the future. Bond funds have expense ratios that vary by fund.

Individual bond issues allow an individual to tailor their purchase for specific financial needs. An investor can search for specific bonds that mature on a certain date and pay a specific amount of interest. The negative of purchasing individual issues is that they generally require at least $50,000 to efficiently invest in. Investors also cannot automatically reinvest the coupon in the individual bond; with mutual funds, an investor can instruct the fund company to invest the coupons back into the bond fund. Purchasing individual bonds may require some personal research or assistance from a financial advisor or broker.

Bond mutual funds can be bought through their sponsoring fund family with no commission or load. On the other hand, individual corporate issues have to be purchased through a broker. Treasury bonds can be bought by individuals directly from the U.S. Treasury through Treasury Direct, which can be accessed on the Internet. Treasury Direct charges no transaction or brokerage fees. The minimum investments are $10,000 for Treasury bills, $5,000 for Treasury notes that mature in less than five years, and $1,000 for Treasury securities that mature in five years or more.

A safe and easy strategy to employ when purchasing individual bonds is "laddering." This is simply buying a series of bonds with a range of maturities, and it spreads the risk over a series of different maturities while allowing you to maintain an average maturity of your choosing. An example of a laddering strategy would be an initial purchase of five Treasury notes, each maturing in the same month over each of the next five years. After each year, an investor would buy a new note maturing five years in the future to replace the expiring issue. This strategy works best with Treasuries because of their liquidity, large supply, and lower dollar requirements compared to other classes of bonds.

Transaction Costs, Yields, and Other Factors

Investors should be mindful of the transaction costs of bonds. Even in bear markets, if you hold laddered Treasury bonds until their maturity, you will never lose any of the principal. Laddering greatly reduces the overall volatility of owning individual bond issues.

Along with bond type, a screening variable that is available on all bond screeners is *yield*. It is usually seen in a few different forms, such as the current yield, the yield to maturity, and the coupon rate. One of the main attractions of bonds is the income they produce. A goal of any rational investor should be to try to maximize return while minimizing risk. Corporate bonds tend to offer the highest yield, while Treasury bonds generally offer the lowest. As we already noted, the highest yields are unfortunately accompanied by the highest degree of risk.

Like equities, the *current yield* is simply the current coupon divided by the current price of the bond. The *coupon rate* is the dollar amount of the actual interest payment. The *yield to maturity* is the rate of return paid on a bond if it is held to its maturity date. It assumes that the coupon paid over the life of the bond is reinvested at the same rate.

Price is another variable that can be mined for on bond screeners. Sometimes screeners have a filter if an investor wants a bond priced at par, a premium, or a discount. A par bond trades at its face value—the amount the issuer will pay at its maturity date. Premium bonds sell for more than the par value. And discount bonds sell for less than their principal value. Some screeners have variables for price below, equal, or above $100. Since the par value for Treasury issues is $100, it is equivalent to filtering for discount or premium bonds.

One main characteristic that bond investors look for is the *time to maturity*. Potential bond investors want to know when they are supposed to get their principal back. All things being equal, bonds with longer maturities are riskier than shorter term bonds. They have wider price swings than those with shorter maturities.

Duration is a measure that is sometimes substituted for time to maturity. It is defined as the weighed term to maturity of a bond's cash flows. It is a better measure of a bond's sensitivity to changes in interest rates than time to maturity because it takes into account the time value of cash flows generated over the life of the bond. Duration is the approximate percentage change for a 100 basis point change in interest rates. A duration of 10 means that for a 100 basis point change in yield, the bond's price will change by roughly 10 percent.

The duration of a coupon bond is always less than its term to maturity. The coupon payments reduce the duration of the bond, and the higher the coupon rate—all else being equal—the lower the bond's duration. For zero coupon bonds, the duration is equal to its term to maturity.

Related to time to maturity and duration, good screeners will have a variable for callable or noncallable bonds. Obviously, if a bond is called, it is not going to reach its maturity date. Callable bonds expose their owners to reinvestment risk since they tend to be called when interest rates are at low levels. Some investors will not purchase callable bonds unless they are offered at big discounts.

Another screening filter for fixed income is debt ratings. The *credit rating* is a way for investors to assess the risk of a bond. It is mainly used with corporate issues. The main rating agencies, Standard & Poor's and Moody's, do their best to assign an appropriate rating for each bond in their coverage universe. It is especially important for an investor to be aware of the distinction between investment grade and noninvestment grade (junk) bonds. The biggest price moves occur when bonds switch between these statuses.

EXAMPLES OF BOND SCREENS

As stated earlier, bond screeners have far fewer variables than equity screeners. There are also much fewer bond screeners available to use. All the bond screens were run on the Yahoo Finance Bond Screener. If possible, investors should do additional research on a bond outputted before investing in it. Furthermore, a bond investor should always be mindful of the transaction costs. Like all the screens in the book, they were run in the first quarter of 2005.

Attractive Corporate Bonds

The screen in Figure 12-3 searches for corporate bonds that have many characteristics viewed as attractive by most investors. Each of the bonds is priced at a discount, with a yield being of at least 5 percent, which is more than twice the yield of the S&P 500. Each of the bonds has a maturity of at least 10 years and a debt rating that is investment grade. Finally, none of the bonds is callable. The bonds returned by the screen are worthy candidates for investors looking to add individual corporate bonds to their portfolios. Since the time this screen was run, some of the bonds that were returned have fallen below investment grade.

Worthwhile California Municipal Bonds

The screen in Figure 12-4 searches for California municipal bonds. California has a high state income tax rate. The bonds selected are all priced at a discount and yield 3 percent or more. As noted before, because of their tax-exempt status, municipal bonds offer lower yields than other types of bonds. Each of the bonds is screened for having at least five years to maturity and for not being callable. Finally, each of the bonds selected is investment grade, having a Standard & Poor's credit rating of

FIGURE 12-3   Attractive corporate bonds.

*Search Criteria	Low Value	High Value
Corporate Bonds		
Price of Bond		$100
Coupon Range (%)	5.00	
Current Yield Range (%)	5.00	
YTM Range (%)	5.00	
Debt Rating Range	BBB	
Callable	No	

Output

Type	Issue	Price of Bond	% Coupon	Maturity	% YTM
Corp	Allstate Corp.	97.28	5.35	June 1, 2033	5.54
Corp	Autozone Inc	98.75	5.50	November 15, 2015	5.65
Corp	Baltimore Gas & Elec Co	96.39	5.20	July 15, 2033	5.45
Corp	Delphi Corp	96.18	7.13	May 1, 2029	7.47
Corp	Ford Mtr Co Del	95.42	6.63	February 15, 2028	7.03
Corp	Ford Mtr Co Del	94.89	6.63	October 1, 2028	7.07
Corp	Ford Mtr Co Del	92.35	6.38	February 1, 2029	7.04
Corp	Ford Mtr Co Del	99.66	7.40	November 1, 2046	7.43
Corp	General Mtr Corp	96.24	6.75	May 1, 2028	7.08
Corp	Marsh & McLennan Cos Inc.	95.82	5.88	August 1, 2033	6.19
Corp	Maytag Corp Medterm Nts Bk Ent	96.05	5.00	May 15, 2015	5.50
Corp	Petro-Canada	96.35	5.35	July 15, 2033	5.61
Corp	Public Svc Elec & Gas Co	91.87	5.00	July 1, 2037	5.54
Corp	South Carolina Elec & Gas Co	99.77	5.30	May 15, 2033	5.32

Issue	% Current Yield	Debt Rating	Callable
Allstate Corp.	5.50	A	No
Autozone Inc	5.57	BBB	No
Baltimore Gas & Elec Co	5.40	A	No
Delphi Corp	7.41	BBB	No
Ford Mtr Co Del	6.94	BBB	No
Ford Mtr Co Del	6.98	BBB	No
Ford Mtr Co Del	6.90	BBB	No
Ford Mtr Co Del	7.43	BBB	No
General Mtr Corp	7.01	BBB	No
Marsh & McLennan Cos Inc.	6.13	BBB	No
Maytag Corp Medterm Nts Bk Ent	5.20	BBB	No
Petro-Canada	5.55	BBB	No
Public Svc Elec & Gas Co	5.44	A	No
South Carolina Elec & Gas Co	5.31	A	No

*Screen was run on Yahoo Finance Bond Screener.

FIGURE 12-4   California municipal bonds.

*Search Criteria	Low Value	High Value
Municipal Bonds		
State of California		
Price		$100
Coupon Range (%)	3.00	
Current Yield Range (%)	3.00	
YTM Range (%)	3.00	
Debt Rating Range	BBB	
Callable	No	
Maturity Range	5 years	

Output

Type	Issue	Price of Bond	% Coupon	% Maturity	% YTM
Muni	California EDL Facs Auth Rev Bds	96.46	3.00	December 1, 2011	3.58
Muni	California Infrastructure & Ec Rev Bds	97.15	3.20	October 1, 2014	3.55
Muni	Kaweah Delta Health Care Dist Rev Bds	98.93	3.50	August 1, 2010	3.71

Type	Issue	% Current Yield	Debt Rating	Callable
Muni	California EDL Facs Auth Rev Bds	3.11	A	No
Muni	California Infrastructure & Ec Rev Bds	3.29	AA	No
Muni	Kaweah Delta Health Care Dist Rev Bds	3.54	A	No

*Screen was run on Yahoo Finance Bond Screener.

FIGURE 12-5   Safe corporate bonds.

*Search Criteria	Low Value	High Value
Corporate Bonds		
Price		
Coupon Range (%)	4.00	
Current Yield Range (%)	4.00	
YTM Range (%)	4.00	
Debt Rating Range	AAA	
Callable	No	
Maturity Range	3 Years	7 Years

Output

Type	Issue	Price of Bond	% Coupon	Maturity	% YTM
Corp	American General Corp	117.08	7.50	August 11, 2010	4.06
Corp	Federal Home Ln Bks	102.00	4.38	August 15, 2011	4.03
Corp	Federal Home Ln Bks	104.89	4.88	November 15, 2011	4.05
Corp	Federal Home Ln Bks	109.30	5.63	November 15, 2011	4.06
Corp	Federal Home Ln Bks Medium	118.31	7.35	June 11, 2011	4.09
Corp	Federal Home Ln Mtg Corp	108.74	5.50	September 15, 2011	4.00
Corp	Federal Natl Mtg Assn	107.76	5.38	November 15, 2011	4.07
Corp	General Electric Cap Corp Mtn Be	114.66	6.88	November 15, 2010	4.05
Corp	General Electric Cap Corp Mtn Be	110.75	6.13	February 22, 2011	4.13
Corp	General Electric Cap Corp Mtn Be	100.90	4.38	November 21, 2011	4.22
Corp	Ralston Purina Co	122.26	9.25	October 15, 2009	4.09

Type	Issue	% Current Yield	Debt Rating	Callable
Corp	American General Corp	6.41	AAA	No
Corp	Federal Home Ln Bks	4.29	AAA	No
Corp	Federal Home Ln Bks	4.65	AAA	No
Corp	Federal Home Ln Bks	5.15	AAA	No
Corp	Federal Home Ln Bks Medium	6.21	AAA	No
Corp	Federal Home Ln Mtg Corp	5.06	AAA	No
Corp	Federal Natl Mtg Assn	4.99	AAA	No
Corp	General Electric Cap Corp Mtn Co	6.00	AAA	No
Corp	General Electric Cap Corp Mtn Co	5.53	AAA	No
Corp	General Electric Cap Corp Mtn Co	4.34	AAA	No
Corp	Ralston Purina Co	7.57	AAA	No

*Screen was run on Yahoo Finance Bond Screener.

BBB or above. Residents of California with high incomes and who are considering adding municipal bonds to their portfolios should consider investing in the bonds selected from this screen. A similar screen can be used to find municipal bonds from other states with high income tax rates.

Safe Corporate Bonds

The screen in Figure 12-5 looks for very safe corporate bonds with decent yields. All the bonds yield 4 percent or more and are not callable. They all have intermediate maturities between three and seven years. Finally, they all have the highest debt rating offered by Standard & Poor's of AAA, which means they are considered very safe. Investors looking for safe and acceptable-yielding corporate bonds may consider some of those outputted by this or similar screens

POINTS TO REMEMBER

▶ Investors are attracted to bonds for four main reasons: (1) diversification, (2) income, (3) total return, and (4) special circumstances.

▶ Specific types of risk for bonds include: default risk, credit risk, credit spread risk, interest rate risk, call risk, and prepayment risk.

▶ Bond screening variables include bond type, yield, price, time to maturity, credit rating, and call status.

▶ Purchasing individual bonds may be costly in terms of transaction costs and/or require large minimum investments.

▶ As an alternative to buying individual bonds, investors might consider bond mutual funds, but again, cost and expenses are an important consideration.

13

REVERSE ENGINEERING

Build a better mousetrap and the world will beat a path to your door.

—Ralph Waldo Emerson

REVERSE ENGINEERING is the process of taking something apart and analyzing its inner workings in detail, usually with the intention of constructing a new program or device that does the same thing better without actually copying anything from the original. It saves time since you don't have to build something from scratch, and in the construction, you can gain a vast amount of knowledge of the intricacies of the item.

The technique of reverse engineering has been used to create software programs and mechanical devices, as well as investment styles, and has been used by businesses to assess competitors' products and by military establishments to analyze their enemies' weapon systems. For example, during World War II the U.S. military did extensive tests on captured German U-Boats and fighter planes to see their inner workings and determine their strengths and weaknesses. In certain industries, products are subject to patent protection, and copying their products is outright illegal.

Reverse engineering has applications to help investors better choose their securities and assess their results. Screening takes variables chosen by the investor to find appropriate securities. Reverse engineering does the opposite: It takes the securities outputted and breaks them down into individual variables. There is nothing illegal about mimicking a successful investor's style or analyzing the factors that drove the outperformance of a portfolio. From time to time investors should look at the individual holdings in their portfolio to see how they are performing compared to their other securities and to relevant benchmarks. They should also look at important and pertinent financial ratios for all the securities they own to make sure they're still worth holding.

Reverse engineering can also be used to break down the results of a screen. The resulting stocks, mutual funds, and/or bonds given as output from a screen can be deconstructed into the characteristics one was searching for in a security, in the hope of finding other potential investment purchases.

The three main uses for reverse engineering in the investment process are:

- Searching for stocks based on bettering the relevant financial statistics of a successful, well-known company.
- Taking a consistently outperforming mutual fund and, based on it, garnering some investment ideas.
- Using an investment style or philosophy of another (usually famous) investor and applying it to find potentially outperforming securities.

To use a sports analogy, many people choose securities based on the name on the back of a jersey instead of that player's overall statistics. A use of reverse engineering is to find stocks or other securities based on others that are highly regarded. In this process, an investor should first determine a company that he or she admires and whose stock is attractively priced. Then choose financial measures that are particularly relevant to the company.

As stated in earlier chapters, some financial ratios and measures are more relevant for stocks in certain sectors. For example, inventory turnover is more pertinent to retailers, and the price-to-book ratio is more useful in evaluating utilities than companies in most of the other sectors. Overall, ratios that incorporate projected numbers are better than historical ratios. Securities appreciate or depreciate based on what happens in the future, not what has occurred in the past. Some of the sources where you can look up a company's financial statistics are: the company's financial statements, Yahoo Finance, a Bloomberg terminal, and Standard & Poor's Research Insight.

After finding the financial ratios for the highly regarded company, put in values on a stock screener that are slight improvements on its ratios. For example, if the admired stock has a forward growth rate of 20 and a forward price/earnings ratio of 15, you might look for an attractive stock for a company in the same subindustry with a forward growth rate above 22 and a forward P/E ratio below 13. A minimum of three relevant ratios that are better than the admired company should be used. Then run the screen and observe the output. This process works best with companies in the same subindustry. If using the subindustry as a variable returns too few companies, try using the wider ranging industry description as a filter. Sometimes the admired stock has such good financial statistics that the reverse engineering screen yields no companies.

In Figure 13-1 the stock of Microsoft (MSFT) is reverse engineered to find other promising Information Technology equities. Arguably, Microsoft has been the most important technology company of the last 20 years, catapulting former CEO Bill Gates, one of its founders, into one of the richest men in the world. The financial ratios used for Microsoft in the screen are as of December 31, 2004. The valuation ratios used are the price/sales and the forward price/earnings ratio. The technology stocks screened for need a price/sales ratio of 7.7 or less and a forward P/E ratio of 19.2 or less, key numbers based upon Microsoft's financial statistics. Two profitability ratios are also used—the outputted technology stocks screened for need to have a gross profit margin of at least 21.3 and a return on equity of at least 11.3, which are also Microsoft's values. Like most of the other screens we've discussed, the technology stocks need to have a price of at least five dollars and a market capitalization of $100 million or more to help weed out extremely small companies and volatile issues. Besides the stock of Microsoft, investors could reverse engineer any public company of their choosing in looking for other potential winning stocks. The same process can be used to look for attractive bonds and mutual funds.

Portfolio managers of large mutual funds and hedge funds usually do not like to reveal much about their strategies and are not fond about the

FIGURE 13-1   Promising IT equities.

*Search Criteria

U.S. Markets	Low Value	High Value
Information Technology Stocks		
Price of Stock	$5	
Market Cap	$100 million	
P/E Projected Nxt FY		19.2
Price/Sales Ratio		7.7
Gross Profit Margin	21.3	
Return on Equity	11.3	

Output

Symbol	Company	Price of Stock	Market Cap in Millions	P/E Projected Nxt FY
DOX	Amdocs Ltd Ord	25.78	5,314	16.6
ATYT	ATI Technologies Inc.	18.22	4,542	14.4
FDC	First Data Corp	41.67	34,580	17.0
FISV	Fiserv Inc.	39.53	7,732	17.9
INTU	Intuit Inc.	41.41	7,762	18.4
LOGI	Logitech Intl S A ADR	54.65	2,383	15.6
STX	Seagate Technology	17.19	7,988	18.8
STK	Storage Technology Corp	32.88	3,504	18.8
SDS	Sungard Data Sys Inc.	27.25	7,872	17.1
TTWO	Take-Two Interactive Software	32.81	1,491	15.3

Symbol	Company	Price/Sales Ratio	Gross Profit Margin	Return on Equity
DOX	Amdocs Ltd Ord	3.1	36.6	15.7
ATYT	ATI Technologies Inc.	2.2	34.9	23.6
FDC	First Data Corp	3.6	39.9	23.0
FISV	Fiserv Inc.	2.1	40.2	15.6
INTU	Intuit Inc.	4.3	79.1	17.9
LOGI	Logitech Intl S A ADR	2.0	32.2	35.5
STX	Seagate Technology	1.4	23.4	21.4
STK	Storage Technology Corp	1.7	45.6	12.6
SDS	Sungard Data Sys Inc.	2.3	55.0	15.8
TTWO	Take-Two Interactive Software	1.3	33.5	11.3

*Screen based on data from Business Week Online Advance Screener.

idea of others reverse engineering their strategies. They fear others will engage in the processes of "free riding" and "front running." Free riding is when an investor blindly copies a portfolio manager's trades. The free rider gets the benefit of the portfolio manager's research and analysis without having to pay them. Front running is when others take positions in a security in advance of a big order by a portfolio manager. This results in the portfolio manager getting less favorable prices for his or her trades. Front running and free riding can hurt a mutual fund's overall return.

Mutual funds are required to reveal their complete holdings a few times during the year in shareholder reports. These reports must be sent to fund owners within 60 days after the end of the reporting period. In them, the fund's investment strategies are discussed. The funds are also required to release their 10 largest percentage holdings quarterly. This type of information can be found on the mutual fund family's Web site, Bloomberg terminals and Web sites such as Yahoo Finance and Morningstar.com. Although, the holdings list may be dated by the time it reaches the public, nonetheless, it is valuable information. There is a good chance that securities that were top 10 holdings when the information was made public are still highly weighted in the fund. Although some funds have very high turnover, 100 percent turnover of a fund's top 10 holdings in a three-month time span is rare.

Investors should only look at the holdings of funds that have good long-term performance records. At a minimum, the funds should have outperformed their benchmark for the past three and five years. Stock market cycles usually last about five years. Ideally, you should use a period of comparison that incorporates a bull and bear market. Looking at funds that have only had only one recent year of great performance is not recommended. Being one of the largest holdings of a top performing mutual fund is certainly not a guarantee that these securities are going to go up in the future, but it does provide a good list of companies for investors to do some further research on for themselves. Good portfolio managers would not have such a large position in a company if they didn't think it had good total return potential.

REVERSE ENGINEERING THE EXPERTS

Reverse engineering can also be used in investing by simulating the investment selections of famous investors. By using the tenets of a famous money manager's philosophy, an investor can find stocks that are similar to those the well-known investor would find attractive. Many star money managers have publicly stated or have written about the factors they look for while making their investment selections. As a caveat, just because a stock fulfills many of the characteristics that a famous investor looks for does not mean that they ever did, would have, or will own the stock in the future. The following paragraphs cite examples of reverse engineering some famous value, GARP, and growth investors.

Benjamin Graham's Investment Parameters

As mentioned earlier, Benjamin Graham is considered the father of security analysis and value investing. Graham's influence on investing is still felt today. His books *Securities Analysis* (which he coauthored with David Dodd) and the *Intelligent Investor* are considered classics by many on Wall Street and should be required reading for anyone interested in investing. He was one of the first financial professionals to stress valuations as a factor in picking stocks. He looked for stocks that he believed provided a margin of safety at their current price. Between 1929 and 1956, a period that encompassed the Great Depression and several major wars, Graham's investments grew an average of about 17 percent per year. Some of the characteristics that he wanted a stock to have were:

- Price/Earnings ratio less than 40 percent of the average P/E over the last five years
- Dividend yield greater than two-thirds of the AAA Corporate bond yield
- Stock price less than two-thirds of the book value
- Current assets greater than twice the value of the current liabilities
- Stock price two-thirds of the net current asset value
- Total debt less than the book value
- Total debt less than twice the value of the net current asset value
- Earnings growth of at least 7 percent annually over the prior 10 years
- Stability of earnings, in that there were no more than two declines of 5 percent or more in the past 10 years

If one were to incorporate all of the above components that Graham would want in a stock screen, it would yield very few if any stocks. The screen in Figure 13-2 is based on some of the principles Graham was looking for in equities. The stocks need to have a high dividend yield and low price-to-book value. The dividend yield needs to be at least

FIGURE 13-2 Screen using tenets favored by Graham..

*Search Criteria

U.S. Markets	Low Value	High Value
Information Technology Stocks		
Price of Stock	$5	
Market Cap	$100 million	
Dividend Yield (%)	3.5	
Price/Book		2
EPS Growth (5-Yr Hist.)	7	
Current Ratio	2	

Output

Symbol	Company	Price of Stock	Market Cap in Millions	Dividend Yield
ARA	Aracruz Celulose S.A. (ADR)	33.67	3,500	6.2
BNG	Benetton Group S.P.A. (ADR)	25.32	2,300	3.6
CV	Central Vermont Public Services Corp.	22.19	270	4.2
HKF	Hancock Fabrics, Inc.	9.25	177	5.2

Symbol	Company	Price/Book	EPS Growth (5-Yr Hist.)	Current Ratio
ARA	Aracruz Celulose S.A. (ADR)	1.9	116.9	2.7
BNG	Benetton Group S.P.A. (ADR)	1.5	47.5	2.2
CV	Central Vermont Public Services Corp.	1.2	51.4	2.8
HKF	Hancock Fabrics, Inc.	1.4	39.4	2.5

*Screen based on data from Fidelity Screener.

3.5 percent (two-thirds of the AAA Corporate bond yield) and a price/book ratio no greater than 2.0, which is less than half of the S&P 500's price/book ratio. The companies also need to have a current ratio of at least 2.0 and a five-year EPS historical growth of at least 7 percent to be selected. The stocks returned by the screen do not mean that Graham would have invested in them, but they do possess some of the characteristics he wanted in the equities he purchased.

Peter Lynch's Investment Advice

Peter Lynch is another widely admired former portfolio manager and author. During his tenure as portfolio manager of the Fidelity Magellan fund, between 1977 and 1990, the fund returned an average annual return of 29 percent and only underperformed the S&P 500 two out of those 13 years (www.streetauthority.com). Under his tenure, Magellan grew from $20 million to $14 billion. Lynch was mainly considered a GARP investor, but he also used qualitative judgments that could not be screened for. He felt that there were great investment opportunities all over and that an investor should concentrate on what they already knew and were familiar with. Some of the quantitative characteristics Lynch sought were:

- Favor stocks with low forward PEG ratios
- Favor strong cash positions
- Avoid companies with high debt-to-equity ratios
- Avoid cyclical and slow growing stocks

In the screen in Figure 13-3 represents many of the factors that Peter Lynch was looking for in a stock. The stocks need to have strong GARP characteristics, with a PEG ratio no higher than 0.75 and a long-term consensus growth estimate greater than or equal to 40. The average company in Zacks database has an average annual long-term growth rate of 16. The stocks also have to possess a strong balance sheet, with a current ratio of at least 2.5 and a debt-to-equity ratio no greater than 2.0.

T. Rowe Price's Tenets

Thomas Rowe Price was a famous growth investor. Early on, he invested in companies such as 3M, Xerox, and Polaroid. The firm he started bearing his name is currently one of the largest mutual fund companies in the

FIGURE 13-3   Screen using tenets favored by Lynch.

*Search Criteria

U.S. Markets	Low Value	High Value
Price of Stock	$5	
Market Cap	$100 million	
Long-term Growth Consensus Est.	40	
PEG Ratio		0.75
Debt/Equity Ratio		2
Current Ratio	2.5	

Output

Symbol	Company	Price of Stock	Market Cap in Millions	Long-Term Growth Consensus Est.
APTM	'Aptimus Inc.	22.10	130	50
CRNT	Ceragon Netwrks	5.44	138	40
IFOX	Infocrossing	16.85	330	40
RVSN	Radvision Ltd.	13.98	280	50
SINA	Sina Corp	25.41	1,283	40
TACT	Transact Tech	18.52	186	40
VASC	Vascular Solutn	9.10	129	50

Symbol	Company	PEG Ratio	Debt/Equity Ratio	Current Ratio
APTM	Aptimus Inc.	0.55	0.00	3.54
CRNT	Ceragon Netwrks	0.68	0.00	2.81
IFOX	Infocrossing	0.49	1.03	3.21
RVSN	Radvision Ltd.	0.61	0.00	2.95
SINA	Sina Corp	0.43	0.44	7.28
TACT	Transact Tech	0.62	0.06	3.25
VASC	Vascular Solutn	0.51	0.00	5.11

*Screen based on data from Zacks Screener.

United States. Price believed in investing in well-managed companies whose earnings and dividends were expected to grow faster than inflation and the overall economy. He also wanted stocks to have characteristics that cannot be screened for, such as a new technology, little competition, and no union problems.

The screen in Figure 13-4 incorporates some of Price's tenets. The stocks need to have high growth while paying a healthy dividend. Each of the stocks has a growth rate of at least 30 percent a year and a dividend yield of at least 2.0. In today's market environment, not many companies can combine these two characteristics.

FIGURE 13-4   Screen using tenets favored by Price.

Search Criteria

U.S. Markets	Low Value	High Value
Price of Stock	$5	
Market Cap	$100 million	
Long-term Growth Consensus Est.	30	
Dividend Yield	2	

Output

Symbol	Company	Price of Stock	Market Cap in Millions	Long-Term Growth Consensus Est.	Dividend Yield
GSL	Global Signal	26.81	1,372	32	5.97
MGPI	MGP Ingredients	7.46	119	30	2.01
SHG	Shinhan Fin-ADR	47.75	7,379	35	2.37
TICC	Tech Invstmt Cp	14.70	149	50	2.99

*Screen based on data from Zacks Screener.

POINTS TO REMEMBER

▶ Reverse engineering is the process of taking something apart and analyzing its parts in detail, with the objective of constructing something better.

▶ Reverse engineering takes the securities returned by a screen and breaks them down into individual variables.

▶ The three main uses for reverse engineering in the investment process are: (1) searching for stocks based on improving upon the relevant financial statistics of a successful company; (2) taking a long-term outperforming mutual fund and, based on it, getting investment ideas; and (3) using an investment style or philosophy of another investor and applying it to find potentially outperforming securities.

▶ When reverse engineering, use a minimum of three relevant ratios that are better than that of the successful company.

▶ Reverse engineering takes advantage of the requirement of mutual funds to release their holdings.

▶ Besides quantitative filters, many famous investors incorporate some subjective and qualitative factors in making investment decisions.

14

PUTTING IT ALL TOGETHER

> It's not the strongest of the species that survive, nor the
> most intelligent, but the one most responsive to change.
>
> —*Charles Darwin*

WHEN IT COMES TO achieving long-term goals, an investor can make a giant mistake by not having a financial plan to save and regularly put money in the market. Debt, especially borrowing that comes with high interest rates, should be kept to a minimum. Interest rates on credit card debt can run 15 percent or more per year, and achieving investment returns of more than this are very difficult to achieve on any investment consistently. Before placing a dime in the financial markets, an investor should have little or no outstanding credit card debt.

A regular savings program should be incorporated in almost every financial plan. If you do not set aside funds to invest for retirement, a child's college tuition, or a down payment on a home, there is little chance when you need money for these important events that you'll be satisfied with how much you've accumulated. Sitting on the sidelines for long periods of time and not investing in some kind of financial assets can have repercussions on many aspects of your life. Once you make the decision to invest in the financial markets, screening is a great tool to get on the right track of finding a host of worthy candidates within an investment class.

ASSET ALLOCATION

Screening for different securities should not be done in isolation from other aspects of an investor's portfolio. An investor should make sure he or she has a diverse group of assets with many different characteristics. In other words, all your eggs shouldn't be in one basket. Look at diversification in terms of all your assets, not just the financial ones. Factors such as whether you own your own home and where you're employed should factor into the way you allocate your assets.

For example, employees should limit their holdings of their company's stock because they already have such a high exposure by working there. If the company runs on hard times and its stock declines, they could not only lose their job, but a good portion of the money they have invested in the company's stock. The former employees at Enron and Worldcom can unfortunately attest to this.

Another major asset that is not a financial security is an investor's home, generally one of an individual's biggest investments. It is an investment that provides a large exposure to factors in the local economy and the overall real estate market. Location and the level of interest rates can have a gigantic impact on the value of physical real estate.

Even though screening is a very early step in the investment process, asset allocation is a critical step that should take place even before you start the process of screening. Asset allocation involves deciding on the mixture of equities, fixed income, and cash in your portfolio. Only after a decision is made concerning what percentage of assets should be in each investment class can you decide which securities to select. Many academic studies have shown that asset allocation is the most important decision investors make in determining their returns. Gary Brinson found that about 90 percent of the returns on a portfolio are tied to asset allocation. His findings were endorsed in 2002 in work done by Roger Ibbotson and Paul Kaplan.

Asset allocation plays such a large role in portfolio returns because individual stocks and bonds are highly correlated with other similar securities of the same asset class. Stocks as a group tend to move together, and bonds collectively tend to move together. As distinct asset classes, stocks and bonds have a much lower degree of correlation with each other.

Investment time horizon and an investor's risk tolerance should be two primary determinants of asset allocation. Investors, however, should also be mindful of the effects inflation can have on investments. High inflation can ravage the purchasing power of a portfolio, especially those that are getting very low long-term returns.

As stated in earlier chapters, younger investors who do not need their money until far out into the future can generally afford to be more aggressive with their assets because they have time on their side. Generally, equities should make up a large part of their portfolio. In more aggressive portfolios, international and small cap stocks should be a significant percentage of the equity portion.

Investors in their retirement years should generally be more conservative, with higher percentages in fixed income and money market funds because they are not earning a salary and, in many cases, they need the income that these investments provide. Also, low-risk and liquid investments should generally make up a considerable part of older people's portfolios because there is a greater chance that they may need money for emergency health care needs. Since people are living longer, retirees should not ignore equities, which have historically offered the best capital appreciation potential and inflation protection.

The most risk-averse investors should have a high percentage of their fixed income allocation in short-term, highly rated bonds and money market funds, where the chance of a loss of principal is remote. No investors, regardless of their situation, should put their money in any investment vehicle with which they do not feel comfortable and that will cause them undue worry.

Besides the two main generic criteria for choosing one's asset breakout—time horizon and risk tolerance—each investor has unique circumstances that should affect his or her allocation decisions. No two investors are exactly alike. Health issues, family status, and income levels are a few of the many examples of special factors that could affect one's choice between the mix of stocks, bonds, and cash in a portfolio. For example, two men might be 45 years old and need very different asset allocations. One might be married to a stay-at-home wife and have three children, with one scheduled to start college next year. The other 45-year-old might be single with no intention of ever getting married, and wants to retire in 10 years to sail around the world. Although they are the same age, these two men should divide the equity, bond, and cash portions of their portfolios in very different ways.

STEPS IN THE SCREENING PROCESS

No matter what the security, the steps in the screening process are similar. They involve:

- Determining your goals and objectives
- Figuring out the characteristics you're looking for in an investment
- Determining the variables and the range of variables that are appropriate
- Running the screen, and rerunning it as needed
- Making a qualitative assessment
- Making an investment decision
- Following up and keeping tabs on the performance and recent news about the investments

Before investors decide to put money in an investment, they should have a clear idea about what they want the money to be used for in the future. Is it for discretionary spending, or is it for important life events such as funding retirement years or a down payment on a home? Knowing what the money is going to be used for helps shape the type of investment vehicle in which the assets should be placed.

Investors should then do a self-evaluation to determine how much risk they are willing to take and when they're going to need the money. Finding investments that can double within a year and offer no risk do not exist. Investors should take a serious look in the mirror and determine how much risk they are willing to take. How would they feel and what type of impact would there be if their investment dropped 20 percent? Fifty percent? One hundred percent? Depending on how much risk they're willing to bear and when they want their money to be used will help determine how it is invested. Generally, investors have a certain overriding need in an investment. Capital appreciation, inflation protection, and tax reduction are a few characteristics individuals may seek for their investments.

At this point the investor can start looking at screeners. Back in the first chapter, in Figure 1-1, there is a list of stock screeners, and in Chapter 11 there's a list of mutual fund screeners in Figure 11-4. An investor should sample a few before deciding which one to use. All the screeners used to run examples of screens throughout the book are acceptable. An investor should look at the screeners to see if there are any preset screens that may be appropriate for the type or style of investments they're looking for. If they set up their own screens, they should verify what the variables mean according to the screener, and how they should be inputted. For example, on many screeners "1" means 1 million in terms of market capitalization. Screeners with filters that allow for a range of values to be inserted are preferable to ones with only absolute filters. The latter are more prone to return securities that have outliers in their financial numbers.

After an investor runs a screen, the results should be downloaded into a spreadsheet program such as Excel, so the data can be easily manipulated. It is important to do a qualitative assessment of the results of a screen. As has been stated before, screens are driven by numbers. A security's financial ratios either pass a filter or they fail; there is no gray area. The strength of screens is that they can give a very good quantitative assessment of a security.

A SUMMARY OF SCREENING AND ITS CONTEXT

Despite the power of screening, certain qualitative factors such as a firm's reputation, its relationship with its suppliers and customers, and potential legal liabilities can never be incorporated in a screen. Investor's should try to do some homework on their own and learn as much about a security before placing any of their money into it. Knowledge can never hurt anyone, and it helps to form a more informed investment decision. An investor should combine the quantitative assessment retrieved from the screen with any qualitative knowledge they can obtain in forming their decision whether to purchase or pass on a security.

Prior to purchase, an investor should feel good about an investment based on its numbers and its recent news. There are so many investment choices, why invest in something that you don't feel comfortable with? An investor should feel confident by combining the quantitative aspect of a screen and their own qualitative assessment that they are making an informed investment decision.

Investors should be cognizant of fees and brokerage costs. If you're doing the legwork of finding suitable securities, why pay high brokerage commissions or loads on mutual funds? If an investor does purchase the security based on the screen, their job is not done. It's necessary to keep track of how the security is performing, which means periodically running the screen that selected the stock to see if it still passes its filters. If it doesn't pass the same screening filters, an investor should evaluate whether they should still hold it.

Screening allows investors to mine for investments in all the major types of securities. Somewhat knowledgeable investors can do it by themselves, without the assistance of a financial professional. Of the methods available for finding suitable investments, screening is an effective and inexpensive way that does not require a large time commitment. More important, it can be used to identify securities that have characteristics an investor is specifically seeking. If you do not want to own individual stocks or bonds, for instance, you can screen for mutual funds or exchange-traded funds that pool different securities into one investment product. There are separate screeners available for stocks, bonds, and mutual funds, which sometimes include exchange-traded funds in their databases.

Investors should be aware that screening for stocks is very different from screening for mutual funds and bonds. The factors that an investor should focus on vary depending on the security type and the investor's specific goals and objectives. For equities, factors such as the forward PEG ratio, profit margins, and annual sales gains are important. For individual bonds, statistics such as yield, credit rating, and term to maturity should be stressed. For mutual funds, costs, manager tenure, and overall long-term performance should be emphasized.

Currently, screening is the most comprehensive for equities. The databases available for screeners are the largest in the equity category, and there are far more screeners for stocks than there are for other types of securities. There are plenty of variables that can be used in a stock screen. An investor searching for stocks can screen using all the major investment styles, including growth, value, and momentum. And Web sites with stock screeners usually also have a host of preset screens for investors who do not want to do the work of setting up their own screens.

In contrast, there are far fewer bond and mutual fund screeners. In the future, we expect there will be a large increase in the number of these types of screeners. Bond and mutual fund screeners also have much fewer variables to select from to filter.

But no matter what type of screener you use, you should have a good understanding of the meaning of the variables being screened. Investors have to be careful because different screeners might have different definitions of a financial ratio or statistic. Before investing in a security based on a screen, try to verify the results of the screen by either looking at a company's financial statements, a mutual fund prospectus, various financial Web sites, or, if need be, getting the aid of a financial advisor. It is possible that a screener's database has errors, and you certainly don't want to put money in a security based on a mistake.

A main mission of Standard & Poor's is to provide analytical insight and assistance so its customers can be more confident in their own financial decisions. By using screening, investors can feel more at ease with their investment selections. Just by engaging in the process, they will become better educated in what they are actually buying. They will be better able to tell the pros and cons of a security as an investment choice.

Successful screens are constantly changing. What is a good screen at one time might be totally inadequate at another. It is mandatory to stay current and watch the markets regularly. There is no magic formula for getting great returns for your investments. Nobody can guarantee that they can beat the market consistently. There is no such thing as an infallible system for beating the market. Despite what some charlatans may claim on television infomercials and in unsolicited e-mails and faxes, no one knows definitely what stocks are going to go up and which are going to drop significantly in the future. If they did, they certainly wouldn't be selling their "unbeatable" schemes to the general public.

Screening cannot guarantee market-beating performance. It can, however, help get you headed in the right direction with a plan of attack. It sets you on the right course to picking stocks based on a strategy. Screening can guarantee that an investor buys investments based on criteria they are specifically looking for in an investment. It certainly beats the hot tip given to someone at a cocktail party or broadcast to millions on an investment-related television show. And as an active process for coming up with investment ideas, rather than a passive one, screening adds discipline and structure to the process of stock, bond, and mutual fund selection. Also, besides helping with the purchase decision, it gives you a mechanism to help you decide whether to sell a security. Most investors find employing a selling discipline harder than employing a buying discipline. Emotions seem to come more into play in the former than the latter.

More than anything else, investing is about probabilities. No single investment is going to be right for all different situations and all different time periods. An investor's job is to find those opportunities where the probabilities of success are strongly in their favor. And screening is an excellent process to help accomplish this.

Being consistently successful at investing is more art than science. The process of screening puts more science into the investing process. The securities selected by a screen need to pass a series of tests to be accepted. If a security doesn't meet one of the criteria set out by the investor, it will not be returned as output by the screen. In other words, pure screening takes the emotional element out of the investment selection process, which in many cases can be a hindrance to performance.

When discussing investing, it's difficult to put definitives on anything. Making statements like "Stocks outperform bonds over the long term" or "Gold is a good hedge against inflation" are generally true, but they're not always true. In investing, there are exceptions to every rule. There are plenty of examples of events in securities markets that went against conventional wisdom. One should use words and expressions like "usually" "generally" and "most of the time" instead of "always" and "100 percent of the time" when discussing investing strategies that successfully work under various scenarios. Times change, and what worked in the past is not necessarily going to work in the future. The only certainty in the securities market is that there will be surprises going forward.

Screening empowers the individual investor. It reduces the need for a broker or financial advisor to give security-picking advice. Screening gives an investor independent and unbiased results. It allows investors to find securities based on criteria they set out, and to prioritize what factors in a security are most important to them. They can become aware of securities that meet their needs, which they previously did not even know existed. It gives investors a better knowledge of the securities they're investing in and an understanding of what characteristics initially attracted them to purchase it. When an investor knows why he or she bought a security, it affords a better standpoint to scrutinize whether the investor should continue to hold, sell, or possibly buy more. Screening periodically helps you form a judgment and leads to a more informed decision.

Screening is not a complicated process. It helps to have some basic knowledge of investment terms and theory. The most important trait, however, is understanding yourself and what you're looking for in an investment, and the desire to try to find it. Screening is like most things in life: With practice and some trial and error, you can become proficient in employing it.

WHAT THE FUTURE MIGHT BRING

Once only available to large brokerage and money management firms, screening is now available to anyone with access to a computer with Internet access. And it is going to become even more widely used and more powerful in the future. As fast as computers are now, they will be even faster, with the capacity to hold more data in even smaller amounts of space. Also, tighter and fairer financial disclosure requirements are starting to occur, and in the future are likely to become even more stringent. Measures such as earnings and book value will be less subject to accounting manipulations, and as a result, investors should be able to get a truer assessment of the relative value of a stock.

In the pooled money area, there will be more lifestyle and target date funds designed for investors who want a certain amount of money on a specific date. Mutual funds will probably have to reveal their holdings more than twice a year and be more specific about their expenses. They will be pressured to lower their fees because of the growing popularity of exchange-traded funds and increased competition within the industry. Furthermore, given the recent illegal and unethical behavior of many mutual fund firms, going forward they will face increased legal scrutiny. Exchange-traded funds will continue to grow and become an even larger segment of the investment marketplace. And sometime in the near future we will probably see active ETFs to go along with the index-based ones that exist today.

Although some mistakes in the databases will still occur, there should be less going forward. Screening should also be more popular as investors become more educated and cost conscious. Ninety dollar commissions on a 100-share stock trade, and the exorbitant loads charged for some mutual funds, are going to be things of the past. In the future, more people will be able to take control of more of their investing dollars than in any period in history. Defined benefit plans are being replaced by defined contribution plans, IRA and Keogh accounts, 529 college savings plans, and there is the possibility that parts of Social Security will be privatized. All of these would require an investor to evaluate investment options. The number of these self-directed options is only going to expand, and the types of financial vehicles and the number and range of securities within them will grow substantially. And the more security choices an investor has, the more valuable the process of screening becomes.

Any way you look at it, the selection of the right investments is still up to the investor. The method that an individual employs to make a successful investment is not often focused on. Any process that is legal, not expensive or time consuming, easy to learn, and makes intuitive sense, like screening, should be looked at. In this book we discussed the how, where, and why to use screening. Don't expect to master screening right away. If you have patience and allocate time to tinker with different screeners, the rewards will be well worth it. There is no better day than today to get started.

Index

ABOUT THE AUTHOR

Michael Kaye, CFA, is a Deputy Portfolio Manager for Standard & Poor's Investment Advisory Services LLC. In this position, Mr. Kaye helps work on portfolios that are subadvised by Standard & Poor's Investment Advisory Services LLC. He is the coauthor of a weekly investment column on Business Week Online's Stock Screening. Prior to joining Standard & Poor's, Mr. Kaye was a senior performance analyst at Citibank and Morgan Stanley Dean Witter.

FREE OFFER—The Oldest and Wisest Investment Newsletter in the Newest and Easiest Format

The *Outlook* is America's oldest continuously published investment advisory newsletter, and now it's available online! Best of all, because you're reading an S&P book, you're entitled to a free 30-day trial. Outlook Online is perfect for both beginners and expert investors alike. The site contains the latest issue of *The Outlook* as well as a searchable archive of the past year's issues. You'll get everything from Standard & Poor's latest individual investment recommendations and economic forecasts to complete portfolios that can help you build wealth. For more than 80 years, *The Outlook* has been identifying the developments that affect stock performance—and making recommendations on when to buy, sell and hold. With Outlook Online you'll also get:

Features on Sectors, Industries and Technical Analysis—These weekly articles will keep you informed about what sectors are poised to outperform, what industries have been on a roll, a where the market may be headed next.

Supervised Master List of Recommended Issues—Standard & Poor's favorites for long-term capital appreciation and superior long-term total return. These groups of stocks have been helping generations of investors build wealth.

Complete Lists of STARS stocks—The highly regarded *Stock Appreciation Ranking System* offers an easy way to pick stocks that Standard & Poor's believes will do best in the near term—six months to one year. Week after week, STARS ranks 1,200 active stocks so you can track changes at a glance.

Platinum and Neural Fair Value Portfolios—Outlook Online also contains detailed information on two more of Standard & Poor's portfolios, both of which have historically outperformed the market by wide margins.

Global Features—Outlook Online is also helpful to investors looking for news and views from abroad. It contains a number of features on both Europe and Asia, including the best picks from S&P's overseas research departments.

Stock and Fund Reports—You'll even get access to 10 free Standard & Poor's reports every month. Whether you're looking for more information on a company or a mutual fund, these reports will help you make informed decisions.

It's simple to activate your free trial to Outlook Online. Just visit the URL below and follow the directions on the screen. No credit card is required and registration will take only a few minutes. To get the best guidance on Wall Street and specific stock recommendations from the experts in the field, just visit us at:

http://www.spoutlookonline.com/ol_mw1.0.asp?ADID=KAY